2.00

D1400121

Art All Year Long

Increase Creativity (and lots of other stuff) Through Color, Shape, Texture, Paint, Glue, Scissors, Clay, and So Much More!

by
Vanessa Countryman
and
Sharon Thompson

Publisher
Key Education Publishing Company, LLC
Minneapolis, Minnesota

CONGRATULATIONS ON YOUR PURCHASE OF A KEY EDUCATION PRODUCT!

The editors at Key Education are former teachers who bring experience, enthusiasm, and quality to each and every product. Thousands of teachers have looked to the staff at Key Education for new and innovative resources to make their work more enjoyable and rewarding. We are committed to developing educational materials that will assist teachers in building a strong and developmentally appropriate curriculum for young children.

PLAN FOR GREAT TEACHING EXPERIENCES WHEN YOU USE EDUCATIONAL MATERIALS FROM KEY EDUCATION PUBLISHING COMPANY, LLC.

Key Education welcomes manuscripts and product ideas from teachers. For a copy of our submission guidelines, please send a self-addressed stamped envelope to:
Key Education Publishing Company, LLC
Acquisitions Department
9601 Newton Avenue South
Minneapolis, Minnesota 55431

Credits
Authors: Vanessa Countryman
      and Sharon Thompson
Publisher: Sherrill B. Flora
Inside Illustrations: Vanessa Countryman
Cover Design: Annette Hollister-Papp
Editors: Audrey Rose, George C. Flora

Copyright Notice
No part of this publication may be reproduced or transmitted by any means (electronic, mechanical, photocopy, recording) or stored in any information storage or retrieval system without the prior written permission of the publisher. Reproducible pages (student activity sheets or patterns) may be duplicated by the classroom teacher for use in the classroom but not for commercial sale. Reproduction for an entire school system is strictly prohibited. For information regarding permission write to: permissions, Key Education Publishing Company, LLC, 9601 Newton Avenue South, Minneapolis, Minnesota 55431.

ISBN: 1-933052-25-2
Art—All Year Long
Copyright © 2006 Key Education Publishing Company, LLC
Minneapolis, Minnesota 55431

Printed in the USA • All rights reserved

Introduction

Try to imagine a world without paintings, sculpture, drawings, or pottery? The importance of art in a child's education is undeniable! Through the experience of art, children can learn more about the world around them; they can learn to be better communicators; they can develop increased motor skills; and they can improve and enhance their reasoning, problem-solving, and other higher-order thinking skills.

Art All Year Long provides projects that help children use and apply various types of media, techniques, and processes—a content standard in art education. These projects can be chosen according to season, holiday, specific instructional theme, special gift-giving projects, or projects that may support a particular area of curriculum or learning game.

Incorporate art into your weekly lesson plans. Provide your students with projects that will help them develop a sense of color, line, shape, form, texture, and space. Not only will your students learn from these art projects and experiences, but they will also have a ton of fun!

Table of Contents

Beginning the School Year Projects
Desk Nameplate..............................5
Apple Name Tag 9
Pencil Desk Plate 10
Easy 3-D Pencil Toppers 12

Fall:
Holiday and Seasonal Projects
Fall Sun Catcher...........................17
Personalized Place Mat 19
Scarecrow Puppet 20
Totem Pole...................................22
Three Ships 3–D Picture 25
Columbus Day Telescope 26
Sandwich Day Stacker Pin 27
Turkey Pin 29
Seasonal Tree Craft 30

Winter:
Holiday and Seasonal Projects
Sparkly Snowflake.........................32
Snowman Doorknob Hanger........33
CD Snowman 34
Winter Snowflake Wreath..............35
Easy Tree Ornament......................37
Handprint Reindeer Magnet..........38
Spinning Tree 39
Pinecone Trees..............................40
Magnetic Picture Frames..............41
Kwanzaa African Masks 43
New Year's Noisemaker.................45
Happy Dragon Toy........................46
Groundhog Day Puppets 48
Valentine Pocket...........................50
Screen Wire Greetings 51

Spring:
Holiday and Seasonal Projects

Tissue Paper Kites............................53
Welcome Spring Blooming Fence ..54
Butterfly Stickups 55
Handprint Window Decorations....56
Thumbprint Rainbow Mobile 57
Rain Sticks 59
Planting Trees.................................60
Handprint Spring Butterfly 61
Animal Babies.................................62
Spring Wreath 63
Bunny Basket 65
Earth Day Hanger 66
Spring Photo Frames 68
Hatching Chick 70
Miniature Maypole 71
Peeking Blossom Basket.................72
Cinco de Mayo Piñata 73
Mother's Day Hand Bouquet 75

Summer:
Holiday and Seasonal Projects

Nature Walk Mobile.......................76
Fireworks Mobile 77

Theme Project:

Birds: Peat Cup Birdhouses 78
Circus: My Circus 79
Circus: Circus Cat Photo Frames....83
Colors: Fun Fruit and Veggies 84
Community Helpers..........................89
Community Helpers:
    Community Vehicles.................95
Dinosaurs: My Dinosaur Book.....100
Farm: My Farm 104
Gifts:
    Helping Hands Coupon Book .108
Gifts: Family Tree 109
Gifts: Handy Clips 110
Gifts: Mosaic Key Holder.............111
Gifts: Zany Pencil Holder 112

Gifts: Frog Paperweight...............113
Insects: Egg Carton Creatures 114
Learning Games:
    Classroom Mailboxes.............115
Learning Games:
    Gone Fishing Game 117
Learning Games: Teddy Bear
    Flash Card Holder 121
Measurement:
    Welcome Ruler and Wreath.....124
Music:
    Shimmering Musical Notes.....127
100 Days:
    One Hundred Day Mask.........129
Patriotism:
    Patriotic Star Wreath..............131
Patriotism:
    Veterans Day Picture Frame....133
Patriotism:
    Star Door Decoration 134
Patriotism: 3-D Patriotic Star 136
Patriotism: Flag Decoration 138
Pets: Pet Shop Memory Match 139
Pets: Pet Shop Pocket...................143
Sealife: Ocean Adventure Tank ...148
Solar System:
    Styrofoam Solar System 151
Telling Time:
    Giant Wristwatch 152
Zoo: My Zoo 154

Desk Nameplate

Start off the school year by helping students learn and remember one another's names. This desk nameplate exercise also provides the students an opportunity to practice learning the letters of their own names and printing or writing them correctly. The nameplate can be attached to the students' desks or to their chairs.

Materials needed:
- white card stock
- bold colored markers
- self-stick clear laminate
- self-stick hook-and-loop tape (Velcro™)
- glue
- scissors
- assorted colored construction paper or felt
- markers or crayons
- small resealable plastic bag
- tape
- *optional:* precut craft foam shapes, an assortment of decorative items, such as pom-poms, sequins, glitter glue, buttons, yarn, chenille stems, etc.

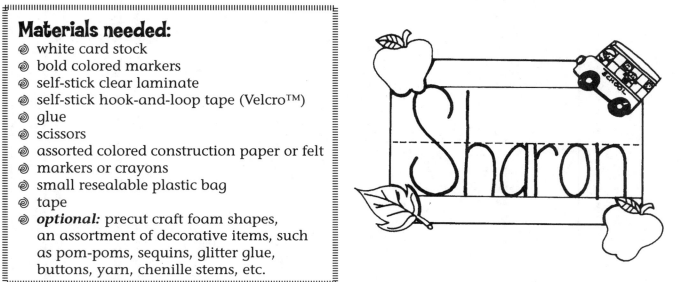

Directions:
1. Reproduce the nameplate on the following page onto white card stock.
2. Write each child's name or let each child write their own name with bold colored markers neatly on the preprinted lines.
3. Cover both sides of the nameplate with clear laminate. Seal the front and back paper sheets together and trim the excess about 1/4 in. (6mm) out from the edge of the name plate.
4. Glue a small piece of self-stick hook-and-loop tape near each corner of the front of the nameplate and let it dry.
5. Reproduce the seasonal patterns (pages 7–8) or any other theme appropriate patterns found in this book onto card stock paper.
6. Cut out the patterns and color with crayons or markers, or use as patterns to cut felt or construction paper shapes. Decorate the shapes with pom poms, sequins, glitter glue, yarn, etc.
7. Cut a small piece of self-stick hook-and-loop tape (opposite of what is on the name plate) and glue to the back of each decoration.
8. Place changeable nameplate decorations that aren't in use in a small resealable plastic bag. Tape the bag of decorations to the back of the nameplate for storage if desired.
9. Tape the nameplate to a desk and decorate.

> **Tip:**
> Make basic nameplates ahead of time for younger children to decorate. Purchase precut felt or foam shapes or cut your own.

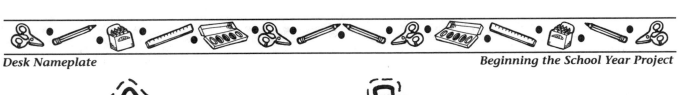

Apple Name Tag

Help ease the stress of trying to remember students' names during the first days of school. This apple name tag will not only help both you and the students learn and remember one another's names, but it will also make an awesome accessory for the children to wear.

Materials needed:
- red and green felt
- assorted pom-poms
- 2 wiggle eyes
- pin fastener
- scissors
- glue
- marker

Directions:
1. Cut red apple and green leaf and stem pattern pieces from the felt.
2. Glue the green stem and leaf to the apple shape.
3. Create a worm by gluing together several pom-poms end to end near the bottom of the apple. Glue the wiggle eyes to the worm's head.
4. Write the child's name on the front of the name tag.
5. Attach a pin fastener near the top on the back of the apple.

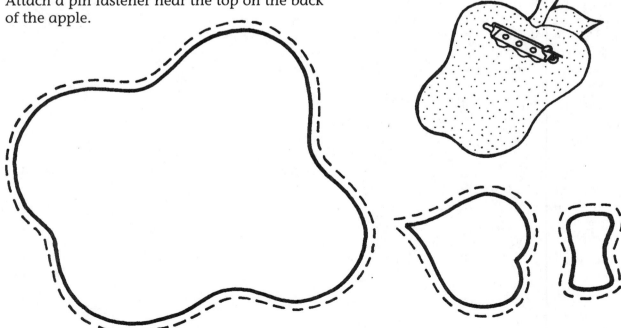

Pencil Desk Plate

It's always important to have desk plates. They not only help to remind you of the students' names, but they give the students a sense of belonging and ownership. This pencil desk plate is simple to create and bolsters the students' pride when attached to their desks.

Materials needed:
- pencil
- pencil pattern
- foil
- yellow, tan, black, and red craft foam
- medium-tip black marker
- glue
- glitter (any color)
- self-stick hook-and-loop tape (Velcro™)

Directions:
1. Trace the pencil pattern onto the yellow (or other desired color) craft foam. Cut the pencil out.
2. Trace the eraser pattern onto the red craft foam. Cut it out and glue it to the end of the pencil shape.
3. Trace the pointed wooden part of the pencil tip pattern onto tan craft foam and cut it out. Glue it to the tip of the yellow pencil.
4. Trace and cut out the tiny pencil lead pattern from the black craft foam and glue it onto the tip of the tan piece.
5. Trace the pattern for the metal pencil top onto foil. Cut it out and glue it next to the red eraser top. Using a real pencil as a guide, draw the lines and dots onto the foil with a black marker.
6. Write (or help the child write) the child's name on the pencil in glue. Sprinkle the desired color glitter on the name and shake off the excess.
7. Cut two strips of magnetic tape 1 in. (25mm) wide and glue or adhere them to the back of each end of the pencil.

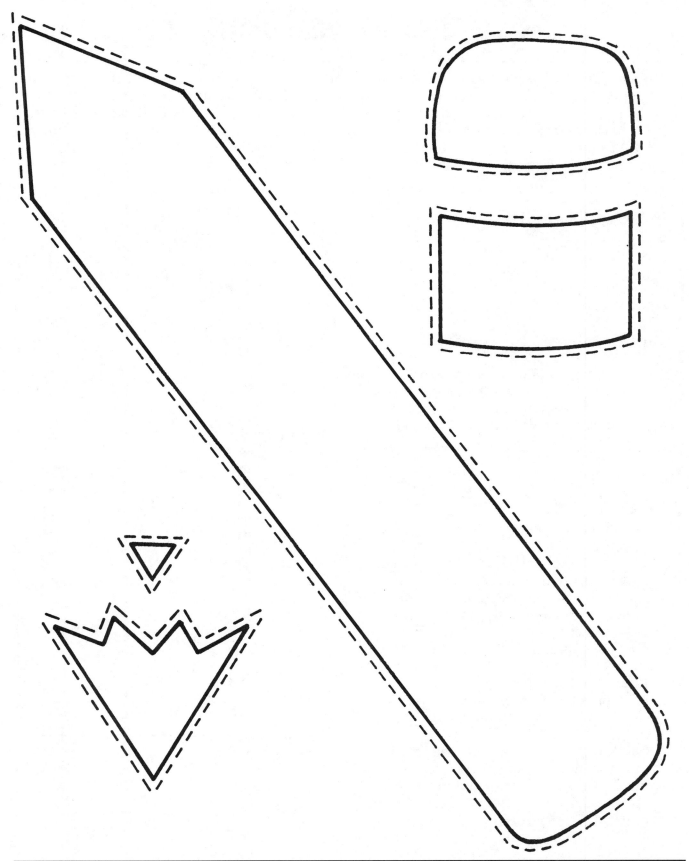

Easy 3-D Pencil Toppers

Children are always thrilled with their new backpacks and pencil boxes filled to the brim with their new school supplies. Take this opportunity to build on this excitement by creating 3-D pencil toppers. There are a number of patterns provided on the following pages so let the children choose their favorites or offer the choice of a ladybug, a star, or a bear now, and make the others for holidays (e.g., Santa—Christmas, turkey—Thanksgiving, etc.)

Materials needed:

- white card stock
- scissors
- glue
- markers
- wiggle eyes
- pencils
- paper clips
- stapler
- an assortment of decorating items: tiny pom-poms, glitter glue, sequins, prepackaged craft foam shapes, felt or construction paper scraps, cotton balls, and chenille stems

Directions:

1. Reproduce the patterns onto card stock paper.
2. Cut out the shapes. Color and decorate.
3. Fold on the dotted lines.
4. Apply glue to the back side of half the image as shown, taking care to leave a bottom section unglued to leave space for the pencil insertion. Glue the front and back together.
5. Insert the pencil.
6. Fold the hands forward and glue together (holding in place with a paper clip until dry).
7. Cut out, color, and decorate the small patterns that go on the pencil-topper hands. Glue the decorated images or packaged precut craft foam shapes to the pencil-holder hands.

glue

Tip:
By using wooden craft sticks instead of pencils, toppers can become instant stick puppets!

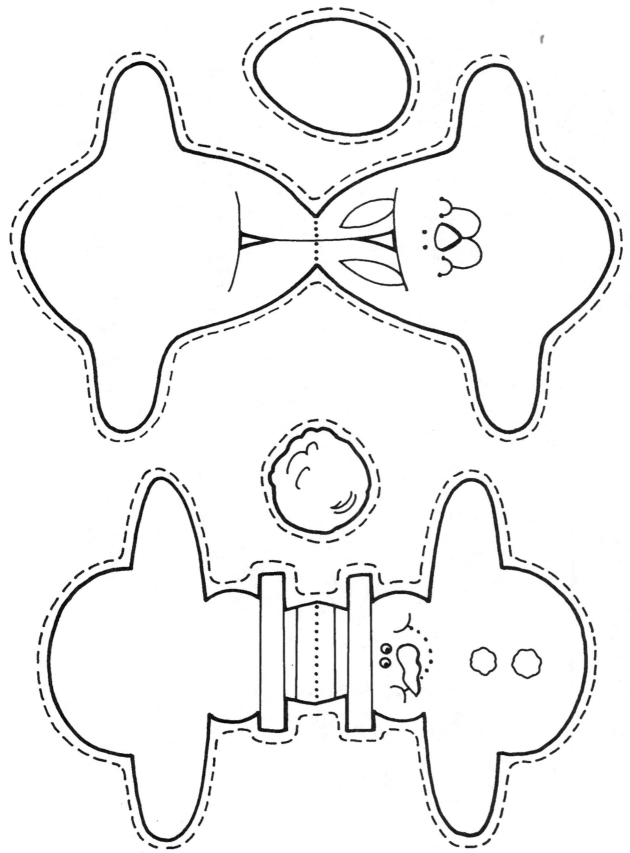

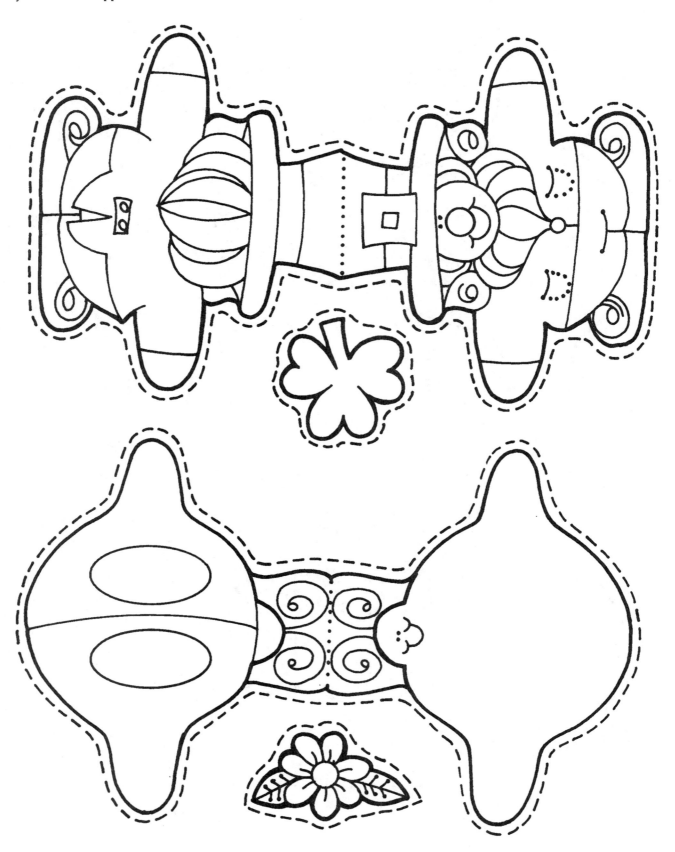

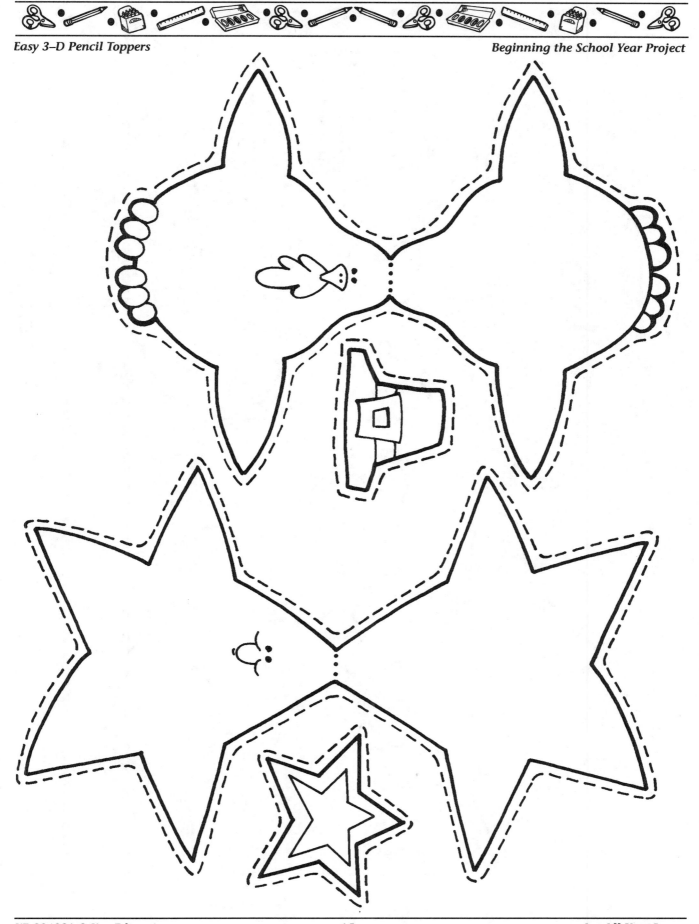

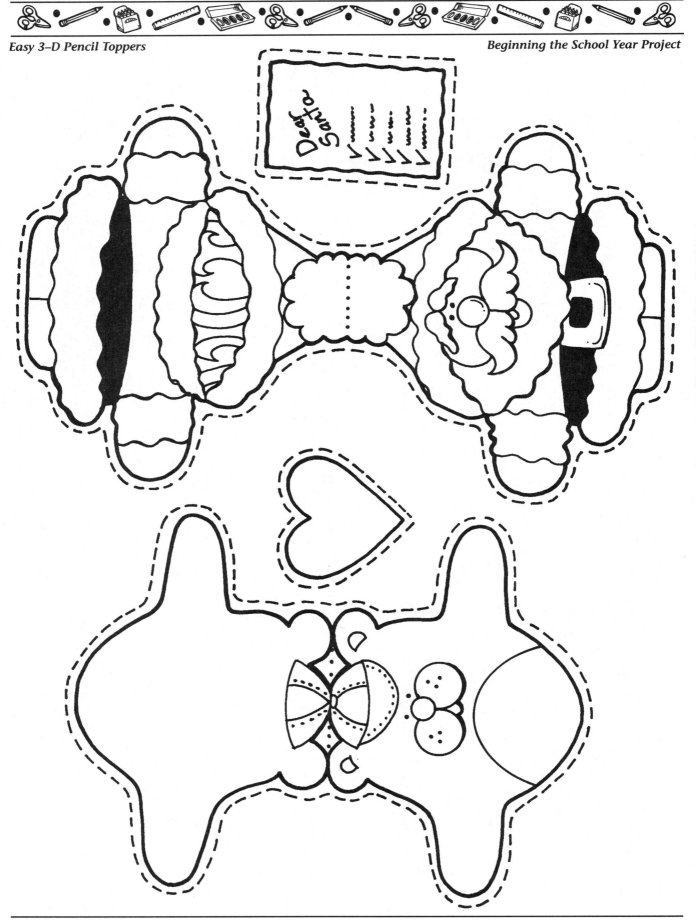

Fall Sun Catcher

Do you recall melted crayon crafts when you were young? They are just as fun and eye-catching now as they were then. Highlight the colors of fall by melting fall colored crayons on waxed paper in one or both of the ways described below.

Materials needed:
- ◎ dried fall leaves or leaf patterns
- ◎ waxed paper
- ◎ small plastic pencil sharpeners
- ◎ old crayon pieces
- ◎ newspapers
- ◎ iron (teacher or adult to assist)
- ◎ ironing board
- ◎ hole punch
- ◎ yarn, cord, or ribbon for hanging

Directions:
1. Let each child choose the colors of crayons and the leaf pattern they wish to use. (Obtain as many plastic pencil sharpeners as possible to reduce the waiting time for children.) Have the children sharpen their crayons, being sure to save the shavings.
2. Lay the leaf or leaf pattern on top of a folded sheet of waxed paper. With a pencil, trace lightly about an inch larger than the leaf. Cut out these two matching shapes from the folded waxed paper.
3. Sprinkle crayon shavings on the waxed paper leaf, making sure to keep shavings away from the edges to insure it seals when ironed.
4. ADULTS: Lay newspapers on an ironing board and set the iron to medium heat. Carefully lay the waxed paper leaf onto the newspaper. Lay the other waxed paper leaf on top. Lay several more newspaper pages on top and iron until the crayon shavings are melted and the pieces of waxed paper stick together. (Check it often as you iron.) Let it cool.
5. Using scissors, carefully trim the edge of the finished leaf. Punch a hole and add a cord for hanging.
6. If you find unsealed edges, dab with a bit of glue or seal with clear tape.

Personalized Place Mat

Fall is a great time of year. When the days are warm and the skies are blue, take your class out for a walk. Talk about how deciduous leaves change colors. Even if you do not live in an area where the leaves change, children can create their own colorful fall place mats. They can display them during mealtimes at home for the whole family to see.

Materials needed:
- assorted fall colors of 9 in. x 12 in. (23 cm x 30 cm) construction paper
- two sheets of clear self-stick laminate *(slightly larger than the 9 in. x 12 in. construction paper)*
- child's photo
- autumn leaf stickers and cutouts
- colorful catalog or magazine photos of fall crops
- white ribbon
- black fine-point permanent marker

Directions:
1. Place a sheet of construction paper on top of a sheet of slightly larger self-stick laminate.
2. Center the photo on the sheet of construction paper.
3. Arrange stickers, leaf cut outs, and fall photos around the child's photo.
4. Write the child's name on the ribbon and then lay it across the bottom of the photo.
5. Slowly and carefully lower the second sheet of self-stick laminate on top of the finished photo arrangement. Make sure that all of the edges are sealed.
6. Trim the self-stick laminate edges, leaving about 1/4 in. (6 mm) beyond the construction paper.

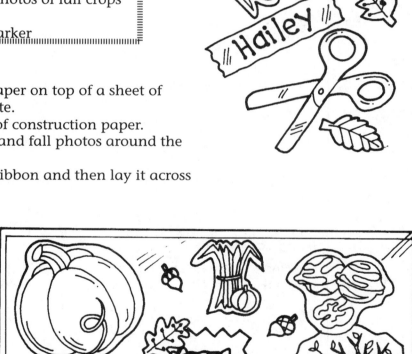

Scarecrow Puppet

Scarecrows seem to have acquired an association with fall. Imagine them standing there among a field full of bright orange pumpkins and drying golden cornstalks, smiling their happy smiles as they chase unwanted crows away. Help the children make scarecrow hand puppets and pretend they are scaring the crows away!

Scarecrow
Materials needed:
- brown paper lunch sack
- assorted colors construction paper
- stapler
- buttons
- scissors or decorative edge scissors
- glue
- tan colored shredded paper
- assorted color markers
- ribbons
- assorted fabric scraps

Directions:
1. Using the pattern provided, trace and cut out the arms from construction paper. Cut the hat from yellow construction paper.
2. Draw a straw texture pattern on the hat with a marker or crayon.
3. Fold the bottom of the bag in half and staple together as shown in the illustration so the bag lays flat.
4. Glue shredded paper to the underside of the brim of the paper hat. Then glue the hat to the top of the paper sack.
5. Glue shredded paper to the end of the sleeves of the shirt. Glue the arms to the center of the puppet as shown. Decorate the shirt with buttons. Cut patches from fabric scraps to form pockets and glue them to the shirt.
6. Using a marker, draw pant legs on the bottom of the bag as shown in the illustration. Cut out fabric patches for the knees and glue them in place. Draw the stitching around the edges of the patches with a black marker.
7. Glue shredded paper on the inside of the sack so it appears to stick out from under the pants.
8. Use markers and buttons to create a face for the scarecrow. Tie a small bow and glue it under the scarecrow's chin.
9. Decorate the hat with dried or artificial flowers.

Crow
Materials needed:
- black and yellow felt or construction paper
- 2 wiggle eyes
- black feathers
- craft stick

Directions:
1. Using the crow pattern as a guide, cut out the crow's body from black felt.
2. Cut a small triangular-shaped beak from yellow felt or paper.
3. Glue the beak, wiggle eyes, and feathers to the crow. Attach a craft stick to the back.

Variation:
Have the children bring used gloves (children's sizes) to class. Glue a crow's body to the end of each finger of the glove. Decorate each crow.

(crow's head)

(scarecrow's hat)

*(arms –
cut two)*

Totem Pole

Any time of year is a good time to teach children about our Native American heritage. Children can learn about the Pacific Northwest Native Americans' tradition of displaying their family's ancestry and social rank by means of totem poles. Share information about the animals that symbolize various things to Native Americans.

Materials needed:
- ◎ totem pole patterns on pages 23–24
- ◎ paper towel or wrapping paper tube
- ◎ white card stock paper
- ◎ construction paper
- ◎ markers
- ◎ crayons
- ◎ scissors
- ◎ glue
- ◎ pencil
- ◎ ruler

Directions:
1. Reproduce the animal head patterns onto card stock.
2. Using the ruler, pencil, and scissors, draw and cut horizontal strips of construction paper the height of the animal heads to fit around the paper tube.
3. Color and cut out the animal heads and glue them onto the construction paper strips or draw your own animal faces on the strips. Finish drawing the animal by adding fins, horns, ears, tails, etc.
4. Glue the construction paper strips with the animals faces around the paper tube.

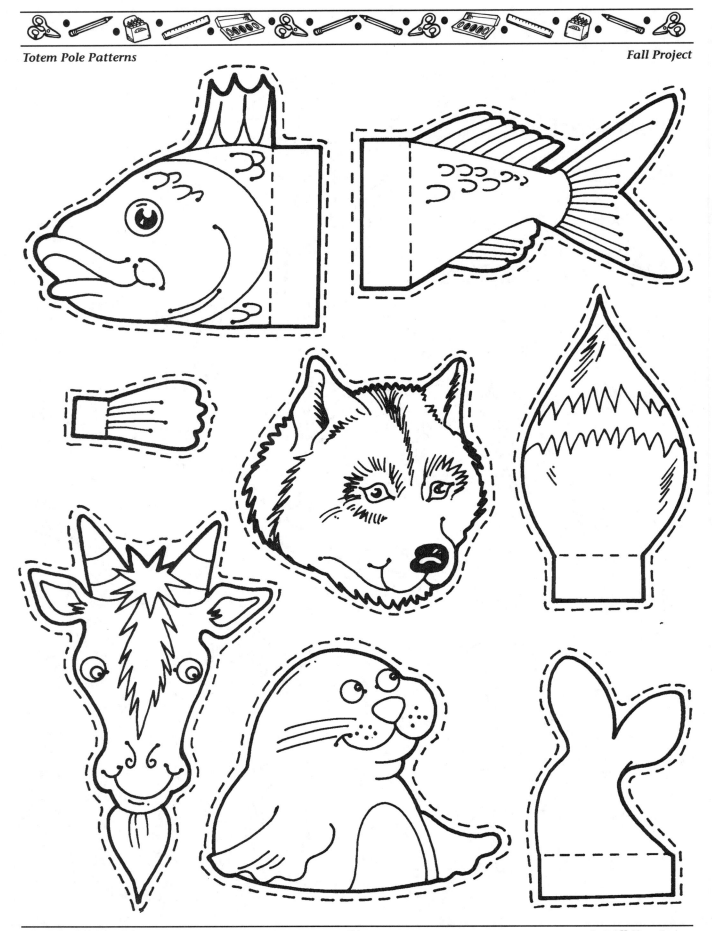

Three Ships 3-D Picture

Teach the children about Christopher Columbus and explain why a special holiday is celebrated in his honor. Share information about the three ships on which Columbus and his crew traveled from Spain—the Niña, the Pinta, and the Santa María. Demonstrate how to use macaroni and a blue marker in this craft to make a picture look like ocean waves. Once the oceans have been created, you are ready to create the ships and set them sailing.

Materials needed:
- ship patterns below
- blue construction paper
- lightweight cardboard 9 in. x 12 in. (23 cm x 30 cm)
- macaroni
- blue marker
- glue
- crayons or assorted markers
- white card stock
- scissors
- blue poster paint

Directions:
1. Reproduce the three ship patterns onto card stock paper.
2. Glue blue construction paper to the cardboard.
3. Draw big waves across the paper with a blue marker.
4. Glue rows of macaroni waves between the blue marker waves.
5. Lightly paint the macaroni with blue poster paint.
6. Color the ship patterns. Cut out the ships and glue them on top of the macaroni for a 3-D look.

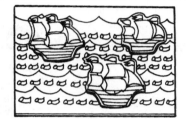

Columbus Day Telescope

After sharing a brief explanation about the travels of Christopher Columbus and how his ships reached the "new world," show your students how to make their very own telescopes. They will love decorating them and looking at one another through them. You may even hear a shout of "Land ho!" as they get into the spirit of exploration.

Materials needed:
- paper towel cardboard tube
- small paper cup
- plastic wrap
- black construction paper and colored scraps
- glue
- masking tape
- stickers

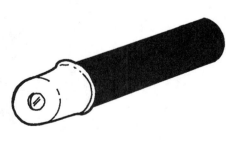

Directions:
1. Use masking tape to affix plastic wrap over one end of the tube.
2. Cover the tube with black construction paper and glue in place.
3. Cut a hole in the bottom of the paper cup.
4. Glue the cup over the plastic-covered end of the paper towel tube.
5. Decorate the telescope with construction paper stars and stickers.

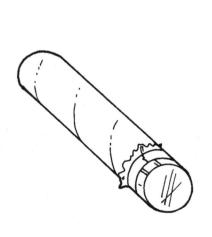

Sandwich Day Stacker Pin

Did you know that the sandwich was invented by John Montague, fourth Earl of Sandwich? Montague was a busy man who did not like to take the time to eat a meal. In order to speed things up, he slapped his meat between two slices of bread. The day celebrated in honor of the sandwich is actually Montague's birthday. He was born on November 3, 1718 in London, England. Celebrate Sandwich Day in your classroom by creating this pin. Perhaps it would be in order to serve some finger sandwiches, too!

Materials needed:
- sandwich patterns on page 28
- craft foam sheets in assorted colors (white, tan, yellow, pink, red, brown, light and dark green)
- pin fastener
- markers in assorted colors
- fine-tip marker for writing names
- scissors and decorative-edged scissors
- paper punch
- glue

Directions:
1. Allow the children to choose the type of sandwich they want to make from the patterns provided. Using the pattern chosen, cut two bread or bun slices for each pin.
2. Let each child create their own unique sandwich by cutting out favorite toppings from colored craft foam sheets (a red circle for tomato, an orange or yellow square for cheese, and a green square for lettuce).
3. Older children may wish to draw details on the ingredient shapes, such as seeds, patterns, or texture. A paper punch can be used to make holes in the yellow or orange craft foam to represent holes in the cheese. Use decorative-edged scissors to cut the green lettuce.
4. Stack and glue each topping with a slice of bread. Glue the second slice of bread on top of the stack.
5. Complete each stacker pin by writing the name of the student on the top slice of bread using the fine-tip marker, and by gluing a pin fastener to the back of the pin.

Tip:
Use fabric paint as ketchup and mustard, small squares of green paper for relish, and white paper pieces for onions.

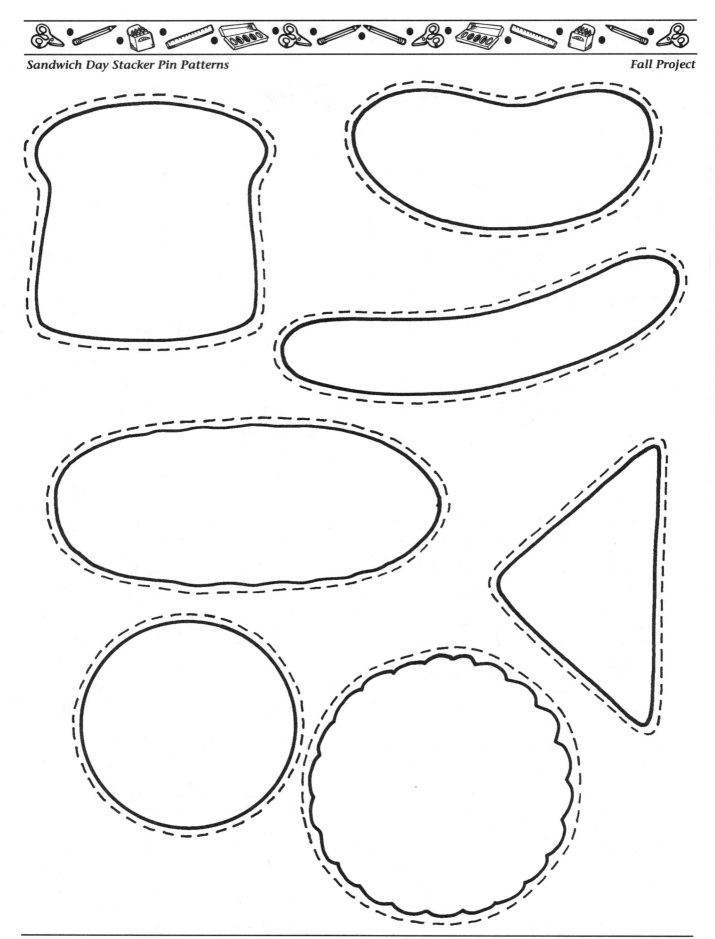

Turkey Pin

There's no better symbol for Thanksgiving than a colorful Tom Turkey. Children can create this cute turkey pin from clay and then baking it in the oven. Add a pin fastener and then give the pin to a friend to share the spirit of the Thanksgiving holiday with someone special.

Materials needed:
- ◎ oven-bake modeling clay (brown, red, and yellow)
- ◎ small black seed beads
- ◎ pin back
- ◎ small colored feathers
- ◎ pencil
- ◎ small square of aluminum foil
- ◎ glue
- ◎ cookie sheet
- ◎ oven

Directions:
1. Form small pieces of brown clay into the shape of an egg. Place the egg shape onto the piece of foil. Press down on the clay so the back flattens slightly.
2. Press two black beads into the clay for eyes.
3. Shape a small beak from yellow clay and a snood from red clay. Press the pieces onto the brown clay to form the face.
4. Using the pencil point, poke a row of holes along the sides and top as shown. These will be holes for inserting the feathers.
5. Place the turkey face and foil onto the cookie sheet. Bake it according to the clay manufacturer's directions. Remove from the oven and let it cool.
6. Dip the ends of the small feathers into glue and place them into the holes around the face.
7. Glue a pin fastener to the back and let dry.

Seasonal Tree Craft

It is always exciting to teach children about the changing seasons—to point out new spring buds, the color of fall leaves, and the uniqueness of each snowflake. Explain how trees reflect the change of seasons through their branches and leaves as your class constructs this fabulous changing tree.

Materials needed:
- small branch or the tree pattern on page 31
- cardboard
- crayons or markers
- soup can
- brown construction paper or wood grain
- self-stick plastic (shelf-paper)
- plaster of paris
- green, brown, and white chenille stems
- green, brown, orange, red, and yellow craft foam
- plastic beads (that will fit on chenille stem) or felt
- cotton balls or quilt batting
- 4 envelopes
- glue
- scissors
- seasonal stickers

Directions:
1. Cover the can with brown construction paper or wood grain self-stick plastic (shelf-paper).
2. Assemble the tree:
   If you do not have an actual tree branch, reproduce the tree pattern onto a sheet of paper and glue it to cardboard. Cut out the tree and color it with crayons or markers. Mix plaster of paris according to directions. Pour the plaster into the soup can and insert the tree branch or the cardboard tree. Let the plaster harden.
3. Using the patterns provided, cut a variety of colored leaves from craft foam. Cut 24 green, 3 brown, 3 orange, 3 red, and 3 yellow.
4. Cut 6 brown, 12 green, and 6 white chenille-stems 2 in. (5 cm) in length.
5. For summer, glue a green leaf to both ends of six green chenille stems. For fall, glue orange, red, brown, and yellow leaves to brown chenille stems. For spring buds, glue a plastic bead to both ends of six green chenille stems. For winter, glue a cotton ball or bit of quilt batting to each end of the white chenille stems.
6. Decorate an envelope for each season with drawings or seasonal stickers. Store the appropriate decorations in the seasonal envelopes when not in use.
7. Wrap the appropriate decorations on the tree branches to show the change of seasons: snow (cotton)—winter, buds (beads)—spring, green leaves—summer, and red, brown, orange, and yellow leaves—fall.

Sparkly Snowflake

It might be a cloudy winter day outside, but your classroom can be bright and sparkly when you hang these glittery snowflakes from your classroom ceiling or along the hallways. Although the sparkly snowflake is a fun and eye-catching craft, the best thing about it is the inexpensive nature of its materials.

Materials needed:

- ⊚ 3 drinking straws
- ⊚ paper towel cardboard tube
- ⊚ 4 sparkly white chenille stems
- ⊚ 24 plastic faceted crystal beads (6mm)
- ⊚ 8 cotton balls
- ⊚ paper punch
- ⊚ scissors
- ⊚ glue
- ⊚ glitter spray (optional)
- ⊚ string for hanging
- ⊚ white tempera paint
- ⊚ paintbrush

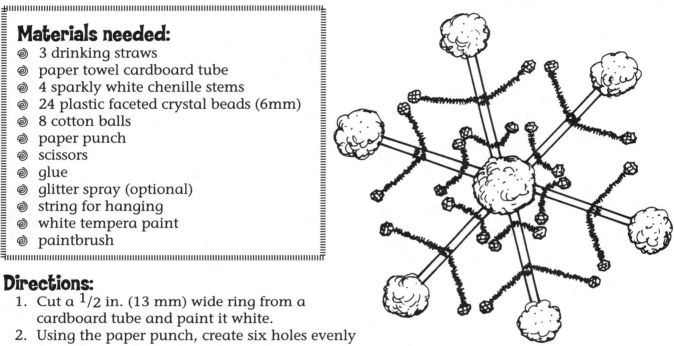

Directions:

1. Cut a $^1/_2$ in. (13 mm) wide ring from a cardboard tube and paint it white.
2. Using the paper punch, create six holes evenly spaced around the paper ring.
3. Thread three straws through the holes in the ring to form the start of the snowflake shape.
4. Cut six 3 in. (7 cm) long chenille stems and six 4 in. (10 cm) long stems.
5. Glue one bead on each end of the chenille stems.
6. Twist one 3 in. (7 cm) long stem near the center of each straw and secure in place with a dab of glue. Next twist a 4 in. (10 cm) long stem halfway between the 3 in. (7 cm) twisted stem and the end of each straw, securing it in place with a dab of glue.
7. Thread a string for hanging through the paper ring.
8. Glue a cotton ball to the center of each side of the cardboard ring. Follow by gluing one cotton ball to the end of each straw and let dry.
9. Optional: Lightly spray the snowflake with glitter glue.

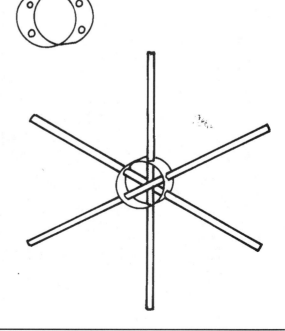

Snowman Doorknob Hanger

Students can welcome others to their homes or rooms when they hang this snowman on their doorknobs. His wiggly eyes, carrot nose, and puffy cheeks will bring a smile to anyone's face. This craft makes a nice addition to the reading of any snow story. Play "Frosty the Snowman" on CD while creating the project, encouraging the children to sing along.

Materials needed:

- jar lid
- red $1/2$ in. (13 mm) to 1 in. (25 mm) wide red ribbon at least 36 in. (90 cm) long
- quilt batting
- 2 wiggle eyes
- 2 large, 2 in. (5 cm) pink pom-poms
- black yarn scraps
- black, green, white and orange felt
- 3 jingle bells
- glue
- scissors
- poster board

Directions:

1. Trace the jar lid onto quilt batting and cut the shape out.
2. Fold the red ribbon in half.
3. Tie a knot 5 in. (13 cm) down from the fold to make a loop.
4. Apply glue around the side of the jar lid. Wrap the ribbon around the glued jar lid sides as shown in the illustration, so the ribbons meet directly across from the knot. Let the glue dry, then tie the two ribbons together where they meet.
5. Glue the quilt batting to the top of the jar lid.
6. Glue the wiggle eyes, an orange felt nose, a black yarn mouth, and 2 pom-pom cheeks at the corners of the mouth to make a face.
7. Using the patterns provided, cut out a black felt hat and green band. Glue the band to the hat and attach the hat to the snowman's head.
8. Tie jingle bells to the ends of the long red ribbons

CD Snowman

Have you ever wondered what to do with all those free internet CDs you get in the mail? Start saving them—they make great crafts like the CD Snowman below. These wiggly snowmen hanging from a high ceiling would nicely decorate a hallway.

Materials needed:
- 3 new or used CDs
- white ribbon
- white paint
- paintbrush
- large buttons
- glue
- orange and black craft foam
- black pom-poms
- raffia
- paper punch
- ribbon or twine

Directions:
1. Paint one side of each CD white and let it dry.
2. Using the pattern on page 36, cut a hat from black craft foam and glue it over the top one-third of the first CD.
3. Glue the CDs in a vertical row on the piece of white ribbon.
4. Cut a carrot nose from orange craft foam.
5. Glue on pom-pom eyes, the carrot nose, and the buttons for a mouth to make the snowman's face.
6. Glue large buttons over the holes in the bottom two CDs.
7. Glue on rolled-up raffia for arms.
8. Punch a hole in the ribbon above the snowman's hat, or in the hat, and insert twine or yarn to serve as a hanger.

Winter Snowflake Wreath

Turn your classroom or a hallway into a winter wonderland when your students create snowflake wreaths—similar, yet uniquely different just like actual snowflakes. Once the snowflakes have graced your hallway or classroom, have the students take them home. The wreaths can be used as great decorations for the front doors of their homes.

Materials needed:
- ◎ snowman patterns on page 36
- ◎ poster board (blue if available)
- ◎ miniature marshmallows
- ◎ glue
- ◎ white ribbon
- ◎ blue and white sequins
- ◎ white copy paper
- ◎ colored markers or crayons
- ◎ paper punch

Directions:
1. Draw a circle 10 in. (25 cm) in diameter with a 6 in. (15 cm) wide center onto blue poster board. If blue poster board is not available, cover the poster board wreath with blue construction paper or paint it with blue tempera paint.
2. Reproduce the face pattern on white paper or let the students create one from paper scraps. Glue the snowman's face to the bottom of the wreath. Using the paper punch, make a hole under the snowman's chin and insert the white ribbon, and then tie a big bow.
3. Create snowflake shapes with marshmallows and glue them around the wreath.
4. Glue blue and white sequins in the spaces between the marshmallow snowflakes.
5. Complete the wreath by punching a hole at the top and attaching a ribbon for hanging.

Easy Tree Ornament

Do you want to make some decorative ornaments for the season but don't have a lot of time? This craft is simple and will only take a few minutes to create. All students can exercise their personal flair for decorating when adding sequins, foam scraps, and ribbon to their trees.

Materials needed:
- 3 in. (7 cm) long narrow green ribbon
- craft stick
- green paper
- sequins
- yellow craft foam scraps
- zigzag or decorative-edged scissors
- glue
- scissors
- gold glitter

Directions:
1. Fold the green ribbon in half and glue to the top of the craft stick.
2. Lay two sheets of green paper together and cut out a tree shape with the decorative-edged scissors—matching the trees together. Glue both tree patterns on the craft stick.
3. Glue sequins on both sides of the tree.
4. Finish the ornament by cutting two stars from yellow craft foam and gluing them to the top of each side of the tree.
5. Using glue and gold glitter, create garland on both sides of the tree.

Handprint Reindeer Magnet

Every child knows that reindeer are a sign of the Christmas season. The reindeer are the ones that bring that jolly old elf Santa to their door, and he's the one who brings the presents! In this activity each child's hand is transformed into one of Santa's reindeer.

Materials needed:
- brown or tan craft foam
- magnetic strips or dots
- paper punch
- red or green ribbon
- jingle bell
- 2 wiggle eyes
- small red pom-pom
- black marker
- glue
- scissors
- pencil

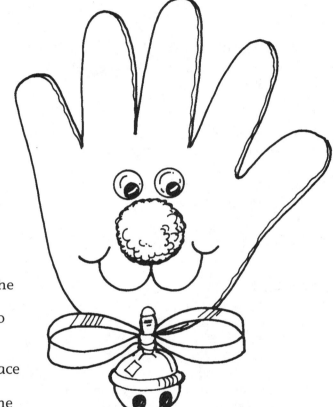

Directions:
1. Trace a handprint onto craft foam and cut the shape out.
2. Glue the wiggle eyes and a pom-pom nose to the center of the palm area.
3. Draw a mouth with the black marker.
4. Punch a hole at the bottom of the reindeer face and attach a bell with green or red ribbon.
5. Glue a magnetic strip or dot to the back of the reindeer face for hanging.

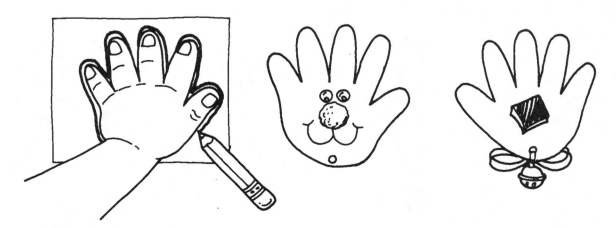

Spinning Tree

Christmas trees abound this time of year. Here's another variation of a Christmas tree craft to try. These spinning trees will look great hanging anywhere in your classroom or school. They will make a nice decorative addition once they go home too. They can also be wrapped and given as Christmas gifts to parents.

Materials needed:
- ◎ 30 in. (76 cm) length of cord
- ◎ green, brown, and yellow construction paper
- ◎ assorted decorative paper scraps
- ◎ sequins
- ◎ glitter
- ◎ glue
- ◎ scissors
- ◎ black markers or crayons

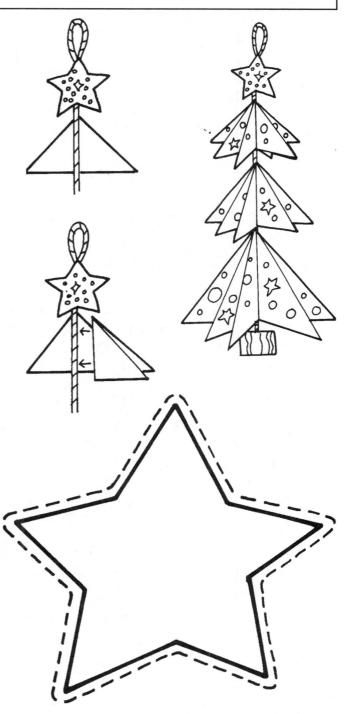

Directions:
1. Cut two stars from yellow paper. Decorate one side of each star with glitter.
2. Tie a loop at one end of the cord. Glue the two stars together below the loop, sandwiching the cord down the center of the stars.
3. Cut three 4 in. (10 cm) squares from green paper. Fold each square in half and cut to make 2 triangles. Lay the triangles flat. Run a line of glue down the center fold and glue on the cord just below the star. Let the glue dry. Run glue down the fold of each of the remaining triangles and attach to the cord as shown. Let the glue dry.
4. Repeat the same processes listed in steps 3 with 6 in. (15 cm) squares, gluing them along the cord directly below the first group. Then repeat step 3 once more with 8 in. (20 cm) squares, gluing them directly below the second group.
5. Finally, cut two matching short tree trunks from brown paper. Draw bark pattern lines on one side of each trunk shape. Glue the trunk shapes together on the cord about 2 in. (5 cm) below the last tree branch group, sandwiching the cord in between the layers.

Pinecone Trees

Pinecones are plentiful in some areas, but there are places where they are difficult to find. If you live in an area where pinecones are difficult to find, they can be purchased in bulk from a local craft store. When decorated, pinecone trees make beautiful centerpieces.

Materials needed:
- pinecones
- green paint
- spray on snow (optional)
- gold foil or paper
- wrapping paper or felt scraps
- glue
- felt
- decorative trim: assorted beads and sequins
- medicine dispenser cup or a large-holed wooden spool
- miniature garland or narrow ribbon

Directions:
1. Paint the pinecones ahead of time or let the children hand paint them.
2. An adult should supervise using the spray on snow. Spray the pinecones and let dry.
3. Decorate the medicine dispenser cup or wooden spool with wrapping paper, felt scraps, and decorative trims to make the tree stand.
4. Run a thick line of glue around the rim of the cup or spool hole and glue the pinecone in place.
5. Decorate the pinecone tree with beads, sequins, miniature garland, or narrow ribbon.
6. Cut a gold star from paper or foil and glue it to the top of the tree.

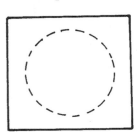 

Tip:
Depending on the size of your pine cone, it may be necessary to cut a circle of lightweight red or green cardboard about 2 in. (5 cm) larger than the base of the cup or spool and glue it to the bottom of the stand to help balance the tree.

Magnetic Picture Frames

These magnetic picture frames are not only fun to make, but they also make wonderful gifts for the holidays. Have a digital camera and printer handy so that you can take and crop pictures of your students that will fit the size of the craft stick frame.

Peppermint Frame
Materials needed:
- 4 craft sticks
- 8 peppermint candies
- glue
- green paint
- magnetic strip
- red craft foam

Directions:
1. Paint the craft sticks green, and then glue them together as shown.
2. Glue the peppermints to the frame.
3. Cut a piece of red craft foam to fit on the back of the frame. Only glue three sides, leaving a space for inserting the photo.

Teddy Bear Frame
Materials needed:
- brown craft foam
- tan craft foam
- small black pom-pom
- small bow
- wiggle eyes
- glue
- scissors
- magnetic strip
- black marker

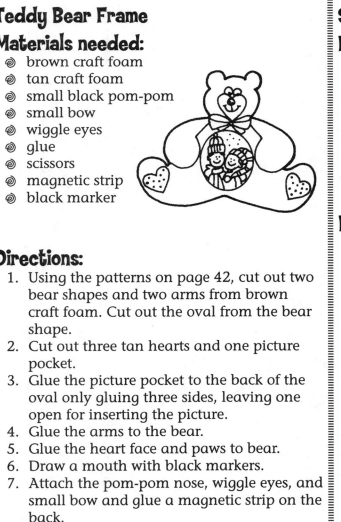

Directions:
1. Using the patterns on page 42, cut out two bear shapes and two arms from brown craft foam. Cut out the oval from the bear shape.
2. Cut out three tan hearts and one picture pocket.
3. Glue the picture pocket to the back of the oval only gluing three sides, leaving one open for inserting the picture.
4. Glue the arms to the bear.
5. Glue the heart face and paws to bear.
6. Draw a mouth with black markers.
7. Attach the pom-pom nose, wiggle eyes, and small bow and glue a magnetic strip on the back.

Snowman Frame
Materials needed:
- 5 craft sticks
- craft foam: green, white, red, and black
- glue
- scissors
- magnetic strip
- markers
- sequins

Directions:
1. Glue the craft sticks together to form a fence.
2. Using the patterns on page 42, cut a green tree, two white snowman bodies, two red mittens, and one black hat from colored craft foam.
3. Glue the tree to the back of the fence.
4. Cut out the 2 in. (5 cm) oval from one shape. Glue together along the head and base to form a picture pocket.
5. Glue mittens and hat to the snowman. Decorate the hat with a sequin band.
6. Draw a snowman face with markers.
7. Glue the snowman to the front of the fence.
8. Attach the magnetic strip to the back.

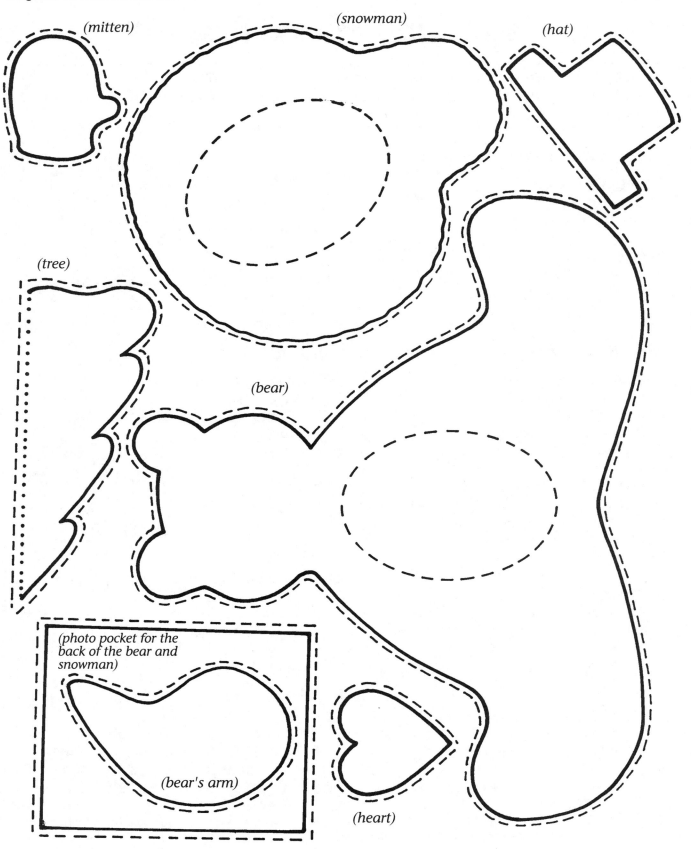

(mitten)

(snowman)

(hat)

(tree)

(bear)

(photo pocket for the back of the bear and snowman)

(bear's arm)

(heart)

Kwanzaa African Masks

The African-American festival of the harvest, Kwanzaa, has been celebrated in the United States since 1966. Teach your class about this African-American celebration of heritage, culture, family, and community while making these creative and expressive masks. Masks are one of the oldest African-American art forms.

Materials needed:
- ◎ pattern on page 44
- ◎ card stock or lightweight cardboard
- ◎ paper punch
- ◎ string
- ◎ markers or crayons
- ◎ construction paper
- ◎ glue
- ◎ yarn, fabric scraps, and tissue paper

Directions:
1. Reproduce the mask pattern or use the pattern as a guide and trace onto lightweight cardboard or a brown paper sack.
2. Cut out the mask shape.
3. Decorate as African animals or create your own exotic tribal design with crayons, markers, or cut out construction paper shapes.
4. Create hair with yarn, tissue paper, or fabric strips.
5. Punch holes on each side as shown and then attach a string to the mask for wearing.

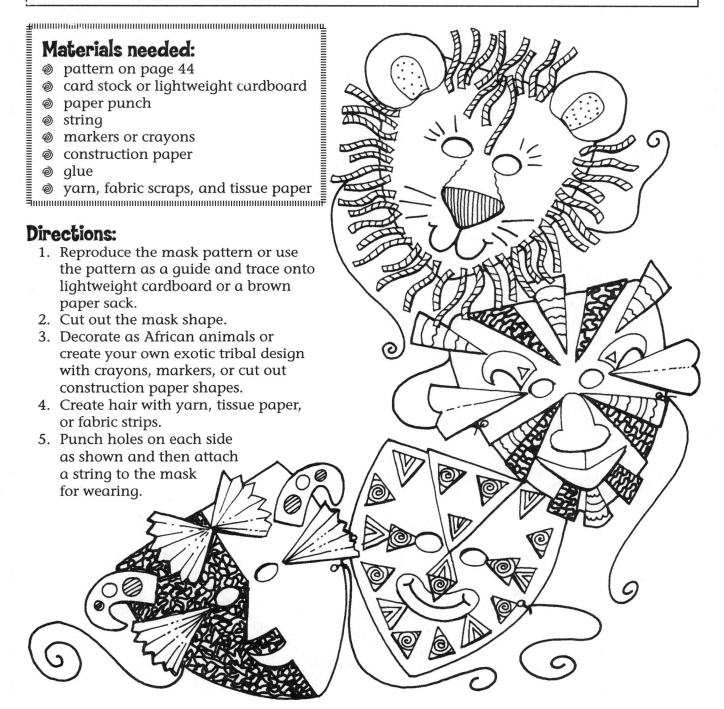

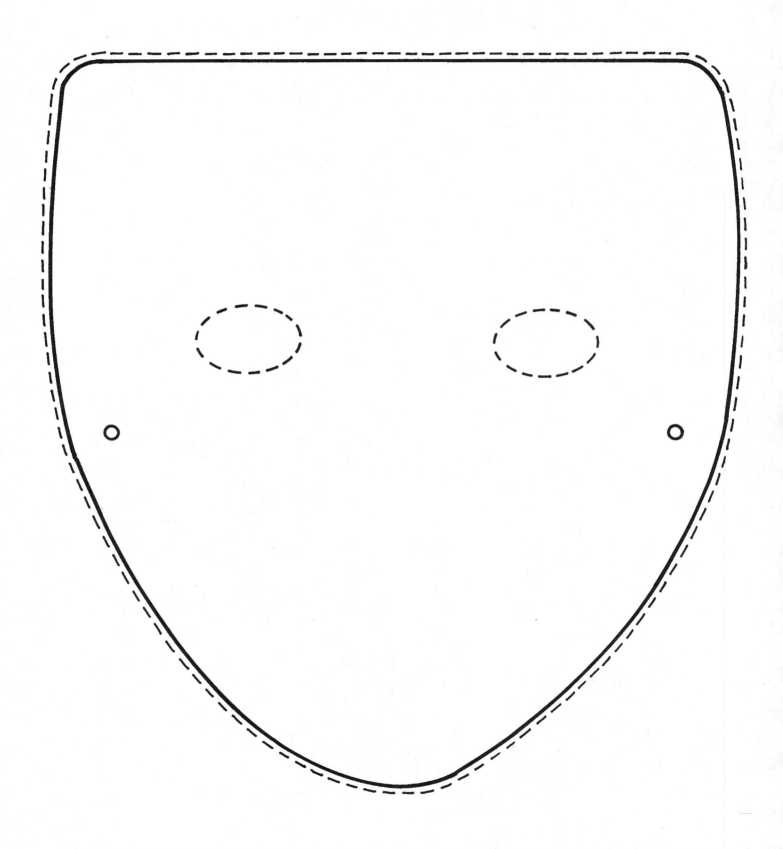

New Year's Noisemaker

How could celebrating New Year's Eve be more fun than by making and shaking this shimmery, sparkly New Year's noisemaker? The embellishments are so eye catching that your students will all be excited to get started on their projects.

Materials needed:

- two small foil pie pans
- paper punch
- silver garland
- five, 8 in. (20 cm) lengths of white cord or yarn
- plastic beads with holes large enough for easy stringing
- white card stock
- star stickers
- silver glitter
- dried beans or macaroni
- glue and scissors

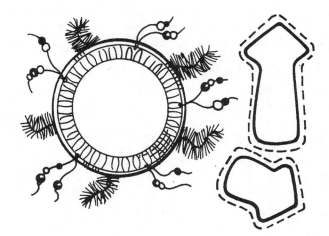

Directions:

1. Reproduce the clock face and hand patterns onto card stock paper. Cut out the patterns and glue the clock face to the bottom of one of the pie pans.
2. Decorate the clock hands with silver glitter and glue to the clock face positioned to show midnight.
3. Place the pie pan rims together and punch five holes through both pie pans, spaced evenly around the rim.
4. Then glue short strips of garland between the holes on one pie pan and let dry.
5. Place the two pan rims together lining up the holes. String an 8 in. (20 cm) cord through each hole and tie the pans together. Before the last hole is tied closed, place a small amount of dried beans or macaroni into the center of the two pans and then finish tying closed.
6. String a few beads onto the cords hanging from the pie pans and knot the ends securely.
7. Complete the festive noisemaker by decorating it with an assortment of star stickers.

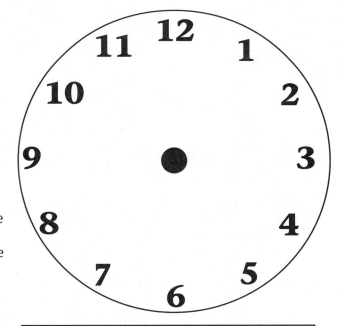

Tip:
This noisemaker could double as a learning time tool by punching a hole through the center of the clock face and pie pan before the pans are tied together. Punch holes in the ends of the clock hands and fasten them to the face of the clock using paper brads.

Happy Dragon Toy

In folklore, dragons have been portrayed as fire-breathing beasts. In China, however, dragons are considered to be friendly creatures that may bring good luck and wealth. A dragon is the main focus at the end of the Chinese New Year's celebration. People carry an enormous paper or silk dragon and parade through the streets in hopes of driving evil from the New Year. Using the directions below, have each child construct their own dragon.

Materials needed:
- dragon patterns on page 47
- paper or styrofoam cups
- pencil
- yarn
- masking tape
- glue
- paper punch
- tissue paper, crepe paper, or construction paper
- giant sequins
- precut craft foam shapes

Directions:
1. Poke holes in the bottoms of six cups with a pencil.
2. Tie a large wooden or pony bead on one end of the yarn. Thread the yarn through the holes. (Wrap a tiny piece of masking tape around the end of the yarn to make threading easier.)
3. Thread the cups onto the yarn as shown in the diagram.
4. Reproduce the dragon patterns on the following pages onto card stock and then color and cut them out. Using a paper punch, create a hole where indicated on the tail. Tie the yarn at the front end of the dragon tail.
5. Decorate the head with strips of colored paper. Draw or create your own dragon eyes from scrap paper. Add ears, a flaming tongue, and additional decorations such as drawing on scales, adding sequins, and yarn hair.
6. Cut strips of colored paper and glue them around the cups to decorate the dragon body. Draw on the scales with markers, add sequins, and precut craft foam shapes to the body.
7. Fold the dragon legs along the fold lines and glue them to the dragon as shown. Decorate the tail with sequins and craft foam shapes.

Groundhog Day Puppets

Use this furry groundhog puppet to explain the tradition of Punxsutawney Phil and the other furry creatures like him that have been used to predict the weather throughout the centuries. The children will love having their very own groundhogs and then being able to determine whether or not the winter season will be extended.

Materials needed:
- ☺ black felt
- ☺ yellow sparkle felt
- ☺ 4 wiggle eyes
- ☺ 1 craft stick
- ☺ large gold sequins
- ☺ 1 cotton ball
- ☺ glue
- ☺ scissors

Groundhog Puppet
Directions:
1. Using the groundhog pattern on page 49, cut one shape from fur fabric and one identical shape from black felt.
2. Run a line of glue around the edge of the black felt groundhog shape as shown. Do not glue along the bottom.
3. Place the fur shape, fur side up, on top of the black felt shape, pressing them together with the palm of your hand.
4. Glue two wiggle eyes and a pom-pom nose on the fur face. First, cut out two small black felt circles a little larger than the eyes. Glue the felt circles on the fur and then glue the eyes to the felt. The eyes will stay attached to the felt better than to the fur.

Sunshine Puppet
Directions:
1. Cut out the sunshine shape and circle from yellow felt.
2. Glue the craft stick to the felt circle. Dab some glue on the cotton ball and place it in the middle of the circle on the craft stick.
3. Run a line of glue around the edge of the circle and glue it to the sunshine shape, pressing together with the palm of your hand. Let the glue dry.
4. Glue the wiggle eyes to the sunshine front. Cut one large gold sequin in half and glue one of the pieces on as a mouth.
5. Glue more gold sequins around the sunshine face for decorations.

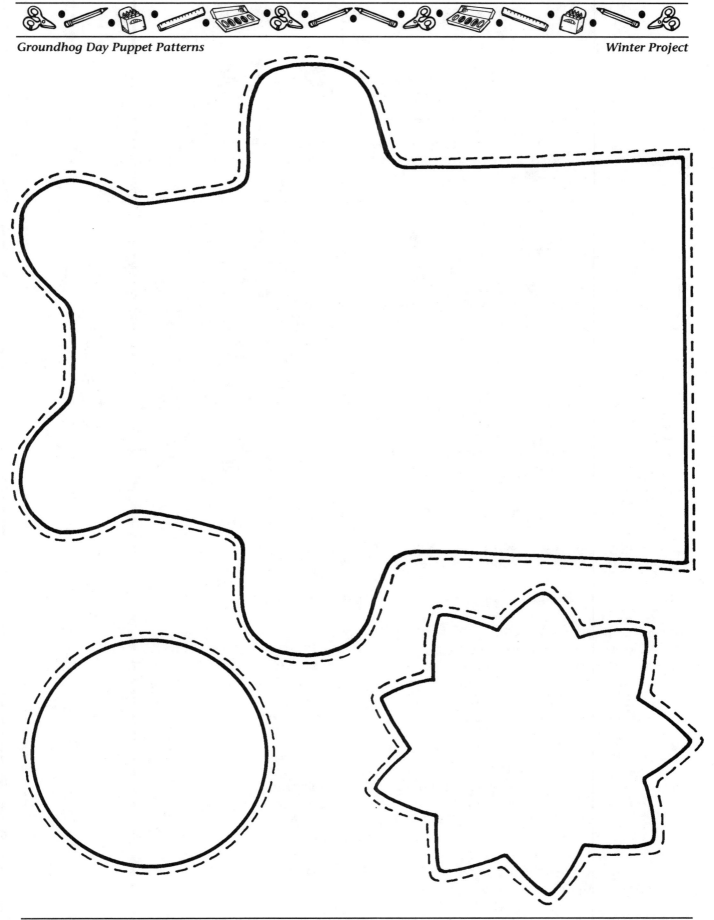

Valentine Pocket

Most primary classrooms still have children create special Valentines for their parents. This adorable candy holder is the perfect Valentine gift for children to make and bring home and share with their parents. Everyone will love the candy treats!

Materials needed:
- one each—9 in. x 9 in. (23 cm x 23 cm) red and pink construction paper
- two 9 in. x 9 in. (23 cm x 23 cm) sheets clear acetate
- pencil
- scissors
- paper punch
- glue
- red, white, or pink yarn
- Valentine candies or treats
- Valentine stickers

Directions:
1. Lay the red and pink construction paper together and fold in half.
2. Lightly draw half a heart along the fold of one side of the stack of papers. Cut along the line to make two matching hearts.
3. Draw a smaller half heart on the folded heart. Cut that heart out.
4. Keep the pink and red heart folded separately and punch holes through both layers along the inside edge of the center of the hearts. This will give the edges a lacy look. Save the little punch-out center shapes for decorations.
5. Glue the hearts to the acetate sheets. When the glue dries, trim away the excess acetate from around the outside edge of the hearts.
6. Lay the two hearts together, acetate side in. Punch evenly spaced holes around the outside edge for lacing.
7. Lace one end of a long piece of yarn through a hole and tie it in place, leaving at least a 6 in. (15 cm) tail. Begin lacing Valentine treats inside the heart and continue lacing to the end. Tie the end of the yarn to the tail from the beginning knot to form a bow.
8. Decorate both sides of the heart with small heart cutouts, leftover paper-punch holes, and Valentine stickers.

Screen Wire Greetings

The painting technique featured here can be used to create cards for any season, but heart patterns are provided so your class can use them to create Valentines. Students can exchange their Valentines in the classroom or take them home to give to friends or relatives.

Materials needed:
- white card stock
- screen wire
- paint smocks or old shirts
- newspapers
- assorted shades of red and pink tempera paint
- toothbrushes for each color of paint

Directions:
1. Fold a piece of card stock in half to create a greeting card.
2. Choose a pattern from page 52 or make one of your own for the card design.
3. Reproduce the pattern onto card stock and cut it out and place it on the greeting card cover.
4. Cover a large work area with newspapers and have the children wear paint smocks or old shirts.
5. Have a partner hold the screen wire about a foot above the card front.
6. After selecting the paint color, dip the toothbrush into the paint. (Thin paint works best.)
7. Run the toothbrush back and forth over the screen to splatter the paint around the pattern, leaving only the inside of the design white.
8. Carefully remove the pattern from the greeting card and let the card dry.
9. Add messages to complete the card.

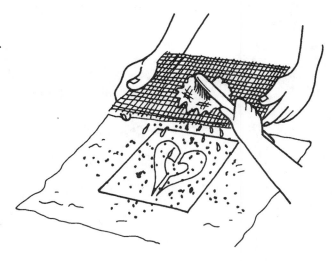

Tissue Paper Kites

Whether March comes in like a lion or a lamb, there will be a time during the month when it will be windy enough to fly kites. The kites featured on this page are not the type that will fly, but they will make colorful classroom decorations and inspire the children to go home and fly their own "real" kites.

Materials needed:
◎ 2 sheets of construction paper
◎ assorted colors of tissue paper
◎ chenille stems
◎ yarn
◎ glue
◎ scissors
◎ tiny pom-poms
◎ fine-point marker

Directions:

1. Lay the two 9 in. x 12 in. (23 cm x 30 cm) sheets of construction paper together. Fold in half lengthwise.
2. Fold in half again, bottom half up as shown.
3. Cut from the bottom right corner to the top left corner.
4. Make another cut as shown about 1 in. (25 mm) from the last cut edge as shown.
5. Unfold the kite shape. Glue a sheet of tissue paper on one shape and trim the outside edge.
6. Glue the chenille stems down the center and across the middle.
7. Glue the other kite shape over the top, sandwiching the chenille stems in between the layers.
8. Punch a hole at both the top and bottom points of the kite.
9. String a yarn loop at the top to serve as a hanger and a long yarn tail at the bottom of the kite.
10. Accordion fold colorful tissue paper rectangles to form bows and tie them along the yarn kite tail.
11. Decorate the kite with tissue paper shapes; flowers, butterflies, and bugs. Add tiny pom-poms for the heads and draw details like legs and smiley faces with a fine-point marker.

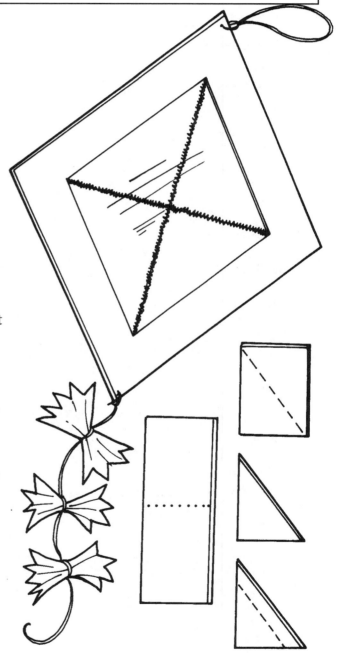

Welcome Spring Blooming Fence

Nothing will welcome spring to your classroom like the *Welcome Spring Blooming Fence!* The fences will add great color and a spring-like touch to your classroom. Later when they are taken home, they will be a bright addition to any kitchen.

Materials needed:
- 6 craft sticks
- white paint
- glue
- artificial flowers
- paint pen
- narrow ribbon

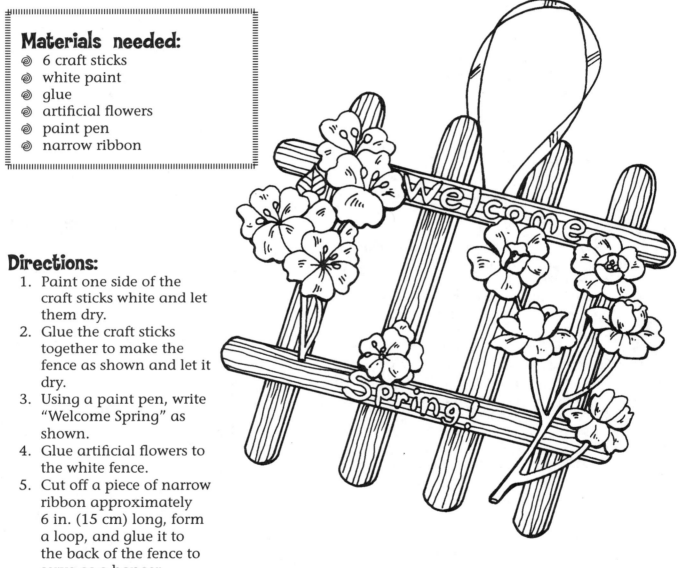

Directions:
1. Paint one side of the craft sticks white and let them dry.
2. Glue the craft sticks together to make the fence as shown and let it dry.
3. Using a paint pen, write "Welcome Spring" as shown.
4. Glue artificial flowers to the white fence.
5. Cut off a piece of narrow ribbon approximately 6 in. (15 cm) long, form a loop, and glue it to the back of the fence to serve as a hanger.

Butterfly Stickups

With this craft children can attempt to capture the beauty of the butterfly. As they paint, they can learn about the intricate patterns on a butterfly's wings. Display photos of various butterflies (monarch, swallowtail, etc.) for the children to see what real butterfly wings look like and then let them be creative with their patterns and colors. These butterfly stickups will make wonderful gifts for mothers, grandmothers, or nursing home residents.

Materials needed:
- butterfly pattern
- scissors
- acetate or plastic sheets *(found at most craft stores)*
- glitter
- glue
- tube paint
- picture hanging putty
- straight pins with large bead heads or chenille stem

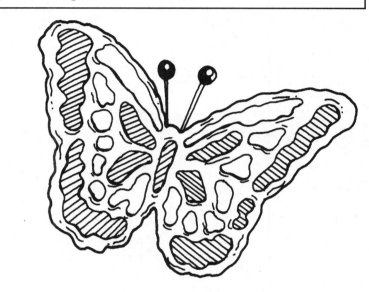

Directions:
1. Trace the butterfly pattern onto flexible acetate or a plastic sheet and cut the shape out.
2. Squeeze on paint outlines and let dry.
3. Fill the blank spaces with glue and then sprinkle with glitter.
4. Stick picture hanging putty onto the back of the butterfly.
5. For antennae: Poke two straight pins with large bead heads or two short pieces of chenille stem into the picture hanging putty. Curl the chenille stems if desired.
6. Stick the butterfly to a window, a wall, or a mirror.

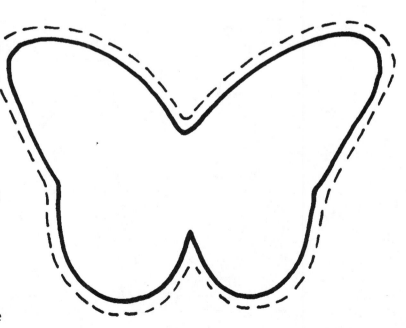

Handprint Window Decorations

Your classroom windows will shout "Spring!" when you display these brightly colored suns and flowers. The thin tissue will "let the sun shine in"! Children will have fun tracing their own hands for their designs and then seeing their creations dancing in their classroom windows.

Materials needed:
- bright-colored tissue paper (blue, green, yellow, pink, and orange)
- scissors
- 5 ft. (1.50 m) length of yarn
- 2 wiggle eyes
- glue
- pencil

Sun Directions:
1. Cut out two 6 in. (15 cm) circles from yellow tissue paper and a piece of yarn that is 2 ft. (61 cm) in length.
2. Glue the two circles together sandwiching about 1 in. (25 mm) of yarn between the shapes as shown.
3. Trace several handprints onto yellow tissue paper and cut out the shapes. Glue them around the edge of the tissue circle to form sun rays.
4. Glue two wiggle eyes and a yarn mouth to the sun burst.

Flower Directions:
1. Cut two 3 in. (7 cm) circles from bright tissue paper and a piece of yarn that is 36 in. (90 cm) in length for each flower.
2. Glue the two circles together one third of the way up the yarn strand, sandwiching the yarn strand in between the flower-center circles.
3. Trace handprints onto tissue paper to form the flower petals and cut them out.
4. Glue the petal handprints to the flower centers.
5. Trace four handprints onto green tissue paper to make the leaves. Glue the tissue paper leaves to both sides of the yarn stem.

Thumbprint Rainbow Mobile

Each of these thumbprint rainbow mobiles will be as unique as the thumbprints used to make them. Discuss fingerprint loops, whirls, and arches and show the children what they look like. (Examples can be found on the Internet.) Explain to the students that each person has a unique set of fingerprints.

Materials needed:
- rainbow pattern on page 58
- newspaper
- white card stock
- tempera paints (red, orange, yellow, green, blue, purple)
- fishing line
- paper punch
- plastic lids
- container of water
- paper towels

Directions:
1. Copy the rainbow pattern onto card stock.
2. Cover the work area with newspaper. Pour paints (one color at a time) in lids for children to dip their thumbs in.
3. Starting at the top of the pattern, make thumbprints all across the top band of the rainbow using the same color paint.
4. Wash the thumbs, change paint colors, and move down to the next line on the rainbow, coloring it with thumbprints. Repeat for all of the bands.
5. After all colors have been added to the rainbow, punch six holes across the bottom of the rainbow. Create a small thumbprint umbrella, flower, raindrop, and ladybug on card stock paper circles. (See examples.) Embellish the thumbprints with marker outlines.
6. Punch a tiny hole in each of the separate pieces of thumbprint art and attach it with fishing line to one of the holes punched in the bottom of the rainbow.

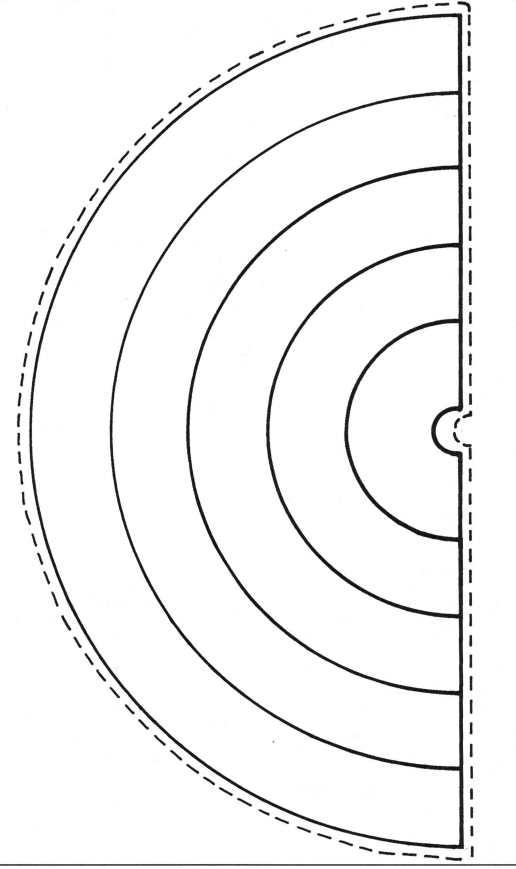

Spring Project

Rain Sticks

When April showers come, children can make their own "rain" indoors. The coiled aluminum foil inside this rain stick gives it an authentic rain-shower sound. Children's natural love of noise will make this craft a big hit!

Materials needed:
- long cardboard tubes
- aluminum foil
- construction paper
- scissors
- glue
- paint
- paintbrushes
- water trays
- glitter
- dried beans or rice
- markers or crayons
- rubber bands

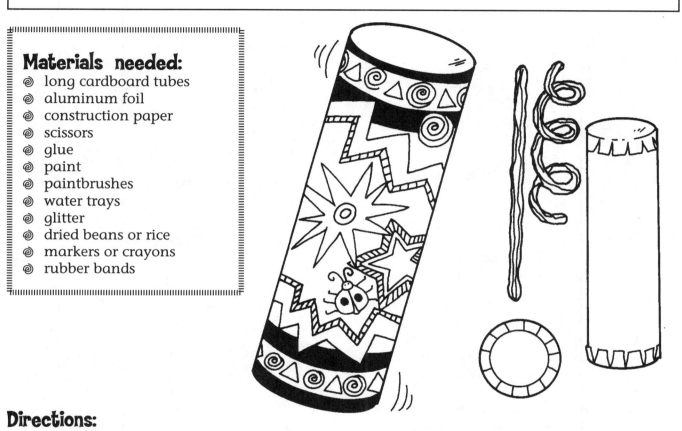

Directions:
1. Tear off approximately an 8 in. (20 cm) length of foil. This piece of foil should be three times longer than the paper tube.
2. Crush the foil into a snake shape. Coil the foil-snake shape as shown and slide it into the paper tube.
3. Trace the ends of the tube onto construction paper. Enlarge the circles about 2 in. (5 cm) in diameter. Carefully cut slits around the outside edge of the circles, stopping the cuts at the center-circle pencil marks. These are the end caps.
4. Center one end cap on one end of the tube. Fold the tabs down over the edge of the tube as shown and glue them in place. Suggestion: Place a rubber band around the glued end until it has dried. Once it is dry, the rubber band can be removed.
5. Pour dried beans or rice into the open end of the tube. Experiment with the amount of beans or rice by holding your hand over the open end of the tube and turning the ends up and down. Add or subtract beans or rice until you produce a sound you like.
6. Cover the open end of the tube with the other end cap as directed in step 4. Cover the tabs on both ends of the rain stick by gluing on pieces of colored construction paper.
7. Complete the rain stick by decorating it with painted designs, markers, and glitter.

Planting Trees

Springtime is the time when everything begins to grow—including new seedlings. Help the students in your classroom learn to appreciate the importance of trees for our environment. Create original and imaginative forests.

Materials needed:
- cardboard
- green construction paper, 9 in. x 12 in. (23 cm x 30 cm)
- green tissue paper
- assorted colors of construction paper and paper scraps
- toilet tissue or paper towel cardboard tubes
- glue
- scissors
- crayons and markers
- small dried and artificial flowers, sticks, twigs, and small pebbles

Directions:
1. Glue the green construction paper sheet to the cardboard. This will be the base.
2. Draw and cut out a small fishpond from blue construction paper and glue it onto the green construction paper.
3. Using assorted paper scraps, cut out fish and glue them to the water. A green turtle, tiny insects, and lily pads may also be added to the scene.
4. To make the forest, create tree trunks by cutting short strips around the base of each cardboard tube and then coloring the tube to look like tree bark. Fold the snipped ends out and glue them to the forest base.
5. Wad sheets of green tissue paper into ball shapes to form the treetops.
6. Cut leaf shapes from green paper and glue them around the tops of the tree trunks. Glue a tissue ball to the top of each trunk, inside the ring of leaves. Glue additional leaves onto each tissue ball.
7. For additional decorations, glue small pebbles, dried and artificial flowers, and small sticks and twigs to the base of the forest. Make small bushes by forming little tissue paper balls and gluing them to the forest floor. Glue paper leaves and artificial flowers to the bushes.

Handprint Spring Butterfly

Start the spring season with a study of butterflies. Teach about how these insects transform through the various stages of life from worm-like woolly caterpillars to beautiful butterflies. As you help each child construct a beautiful butterfly, identify its body parts: head, antennae, wings, legs, and eyes. For older students, talk about the insect's body in more detail, such as explaining the compound eye or the mouth parts. Also talk about the egg, larva, and pupa stages of metamorphosis.

Materials needed:
- construction paper
- pencil
- pom-poms
- chenille stem
- wiggle eyes
- sequins
- glue
- black marker
- ribbon
- paper punch

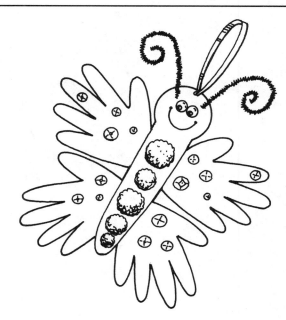

Directions:
1. Using the pattern below, cut out the body shape from construction paper.
2. Cut two 3 in. (7 cm) lengths of chenille stem to make the antennas and glue them to the head. After the glue dries, curl the ends.
3. Glue the eyes on the head and draw a smile with black marker.
4. Glue a row of pom-poms along the body.
5. Trace four handprints onto construction paper and cut out the shapes to use as the wings. Decorate the wings with sequins.
6. Glue the hand shapes to the back of the body to form the insect's wings.
7. Punch a hole at the top of the head and tie on a ribbon to serve as a hanger.

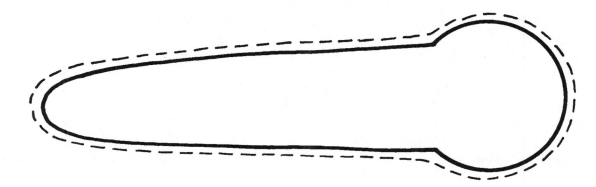

Animal Babies

Create these animal babies out of wooden hearts, cups, and spools. Use them during a discussion about spring and how animals often bear their young during this season.

Baby Sheep

Materials needed:

- wooden disk
- 1 in. (25 mm) styrofoam ball
- black paint
- paintbrush
- cotton batting
- wiggle eyes
- black felt
- glue
- tiny white pom-pom
- tiny pink pom-pom

Directions:

1. Paint the wooden disk black.
2. Glue styrofoam ball to the top of the disk.
3. Glue the cotton batting onto the ball.
4. Glue on the two wiggle eyes, the pink pom-pom nose, and the white pom-pom tail. Cut out two small oval ears from black felt and glue them on the sides of the sheep.

Baby Bunny

Materials needed:

- wooden heart
- wooden cup (flared lip)
- paintbrush
- white acrylic paint
- white card stock
- glue
- scissors
- ear patterns
- tiny pink pom-pom
- white pom-pom
- wiggle eyes
- black fine-tipped marker

Directions:

1. Paint the wooden heart and cup white. Paint both sides of the heart, but only the outside of the cup. Let dry.
2. Glue the cup upside down on top of the heart. Set it aside to dry.
3. Using the ear patterns provided, cut outer ears from white card stock and inner ears from pink felt. Glue the finished ears to the top of the cup.
4. Glue on the 2 wiggle eyes and a pink pom-pom nose.
5. Use the black fine-tipped marker to add whiskers to the face.
6. Glue a white pom-pom onto the back of the cup for a tail.

Baby Chick

Materials needed:

- orange and yellow acrylic paint
- wooden heart
- wooden ball
- glue
- paintbrush
- orange felt
- scissors
- wiggle eyes
- yellow feathers

Directions:

1. Paint the entire wooden heart orange and the wooden ball yellow. Let the paint dry.
2. Glue the ball to the wooden heart.
3. Glue a small yellow feather to each side of the yellow ball for the wings.
4. Cut out a diamond-shaped piece of orange felt for the beak. Add a dab of glue to its center and attach the felt to the middle of the wooden ball between the feathers.
5. Glue the wiggle eyes to the wooden ball just above the beak.

Spring Wreath

Nothing is more endearing to parents than having their children bring home crafts made "with their own hands." This wreath, that is both "handmade" and "made with hands," can be a keepsake for years to come. Choose colorful pastels for a true spring-like look.

Materials needed:
- egg patterns on page 64
- pastel-colored construction paper
- pencil
- scissors
- white card stock
- markers or crayons
- glitter markers
- wide pastel-colored ribbon
- cord
- paper punch
- glue

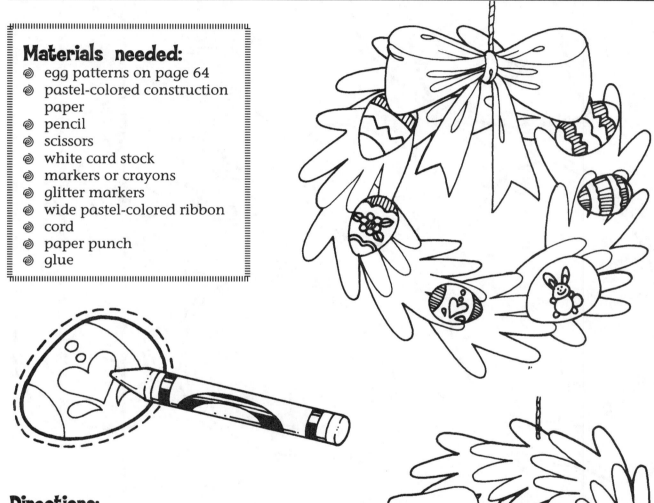

Directions:
1. Reproduce egg patterns onto white card stock.
2. Decorate the eggs by using markers, crayons, and glitter markers.
3. Trace at least 10 handprints onto the pastel-colored construction paper and cut them out.
4. Glue the palm prints together in the shape of a wreath. Then glue the eggs to the wreath.
5. Punch a hole at the top of the wreath and attach a cord to serve as a hanger.
6. Tie a large bow with pastel ribbon and glue it to the top center of the wreath.

Spring Project

Bunny Basket

Are you in need of a Spring party favor? This dainty little basket can be created by the children and filled with small candies. Not only will the baskets look great on the children's desks when the parents arrive, but they will make cute decorations at home for years to come

Materials needed:

- ◎ $3/4$ in. to 1 in. Styrofoam ball (19 mm x 25 mm)
- ◎ wiggle eyes
- ◎ tiny pink pom-pom
- ◎ pink and white felt
- ◎ medicine dispenser cup
- ◎ 6 in. (15 cm) long pastel chenille stem
- ◎ decorative grass
- ◎ tiny dried or artificial flowers
- ◎ glue
- ◎ pastel ribbon
- ◎ seasonal stickers
- ◎ small treats
- ◎ scissors

Directions:

1. Cut a slit halfway through the Styrofoam ball. Slide the ball onto the edge of the cup as shown, gluing it in place.
2. Cut the white ears and pink centers from felt using the patterns on this page. Glue the pink centers to the white ears. Attach the completed ears, wiggle eyes, and pom pom nose to the bunny as shown.
3. Shape the chenille stem to form a handle, gluing the ends onto the inside of the cup (basket).
4. Using the pastel ribbon, tie a bow on the handle. Glue dried or artificial flowers to the bow knot.
5. Decorate the bunny basket with seasonal stickers and fill it with decorative grass and small treats.

Earth Day Hanger

Your students can show that they have the spirit of Earth Day when they create this handsome Earth Day hanger. Although it is nice to plan outdoor activities for Earth Day, the weather may not always be cooperative. This craft activity can become a great indoor way to celebrate Earth Day! Use the finished products to decorate your classroom or hallways.

Materials needed:

- patterns on page 67
- 15 in. (38 cm) length of narrow white ribbon
- 5 in. (13 cm) length of 1 in. (25 mm) wide white ribbon
- card stock
- glue
- yellow, light blue, and green craft foam
- black fine-tip marker
- green paint pen
- wiggle eyes
- scissors

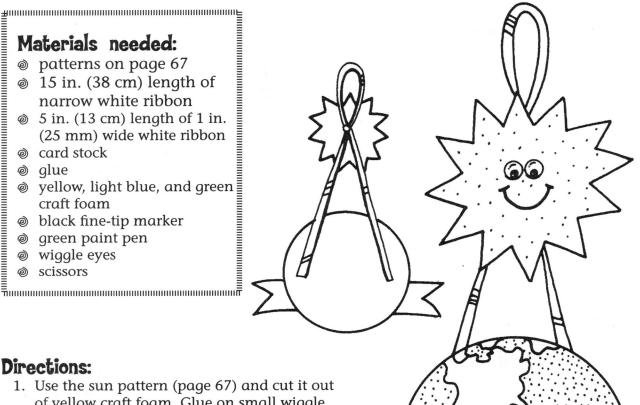

Directions:

1. Use the sun pattern (page 67) and cut it out of yellow craft foam. Glue on small wiggle eyes and draw a smile with fine-tip marker.
2. Reproduce the Earth pattern (page 67) on card stock for each student.
3. Color the land on the Earth green and the oceans blue.
4. Write "Earth Day" on the wide white ribbon and glue it across the bottom portion of the earth.
5. Fold the narrow white ribbon in half.
6. Tie a knot 5 in. (13 cm) down from the fold.
7. Glue the sunburst over the knot.
8. Glue the ends of the white ribbon to the back of the earth as shown.

Spring Photo Frames

Catch some rays by creating these sun-catcher photo frames and then hanging them in your classroom windows for the children to enjoy while viewing their photographs. (Once the catchers go home, they should not be left in the window indefinitely as the photos could fade.)

Materials needed:
- photo frame patterns on page 69
- colored card stock
- colored tissue paper or cellophane
- 2 pom-poms
- string
- paper punch
- scissors
- glue
- chenille stem

Directions:
1. Reproduce two copies of the same pattern (either the butterfly or flower) onto card stock paper for each photo frame.
2. Cut out along all of the dash lines on the pattern.
3. Run a line of glue along the inside edge of each cutout. Place a sheet of tissue paper or cellophane on top of one glued cutout. Position the other cutout, glue side down on top of the stack, making certain the edges match.
4. For the butterfly frame, glue the photo on its head.
5. Form the chenille to make the antennae and glue them to the back of the photograph. Dip 2 pom-poms in glue and attach to the ends of the antennae. Decorate the frame with large assorted shaped sequins. For the flower, glue the photo to the center of the flower. Crumple small pieces of tissue paper into little balls and glue them to the center of the flower along with some large sequins to frame the child's photo.

Hatching Chick

This adorable and easy-to-make hatching chick can be used in conjunction with a unit on spring babies. Every child will be happy to display their hatching chick for all to see! Have a discussion about the various names for baby animals: kit, cub, pup, kid, calf, joey, etc.

Materials needed:
◉ small round or egg-shaped styrofoam ball (cut in half)
◉ yellow pom-pom
◉ 2 wiggle eyes
◉ orange felt
◉ brown paper sack

(figure 1)

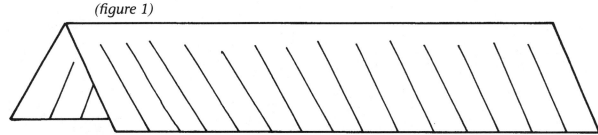

Directions:
1. Cut a strip of brown paper sack 4 in. (10 cm) wide and long enough to wrap around the base of the foam egg shape.
2. Fold the paper strip in half and clip along the edges close to the fold as shown in figure 1.
3. Wrap the paper sack into a nest shape to fit the base of the egg and overlapping the ends. Staple the overlapped ends together. Crumple the nest strips to give it more fullness and glue the base of the egg to the nest.
4. Glue the yellow pom-pom chick to the top center of the egg. Then glue on two wiggle eyes and a small orange felt mouth to the pom-pom.

Miniature Maypole

You may be hard pressed to find a child that has ever seen an actual Maypole, or for that matter, even knows what one is. Take this opportunity to create miniature Maypoles and explain how they were once used to celebrate May Day. Participants, each holding a colorful streamer, danced in a circle around the Maypole until it was totally covered with the brightly colored streamers.

Materials needed:
- ◎ dowel rod
- ◎ glue
- ◎ various colors of tissue paper
- ◎ Styrofoam or wooden ball
- ◎ small silk flower
- ◎ pony bead

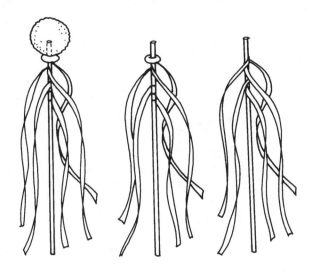

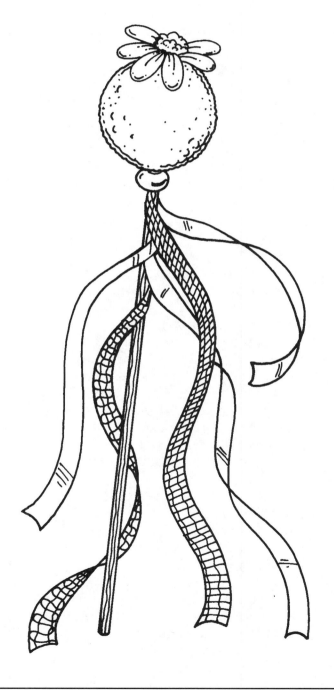

Directions:
1. Cut thin strips of different colors of tissue paper the length of the dowel rod to make the streamers. Glue one end of each streamer to the top edge of the dowel rod.
2. Glue a pony bead to the very top of the dowel rod. Let the glue dry.
3. Glue a small Styrofoam ball to the top of the pony bead and let dry.
4. Glue a silk flower to the top of the foam ball.

Peeking Blossom Basket

Do not let celebrating May Day by delivering baskets of goodies become a thing of the past. Teach children how to create their own May Day baskets, then add a few candy treats or flowers and secretly deliver them to a friend. Explain the fine art of secret delivery by knocking or ringing the bell and then hiding to watch the look of surprise on the recipient's face. Remind the children that they should give their baskets only to people they know well and have their parents with them when they make the deliveries.

Materials needed:
- 12 in. (30 cm) ribbon
- large wiggle eyes
- craft foam
- glue
- markers
- large sequins
- artificial or dried flowers or small treats

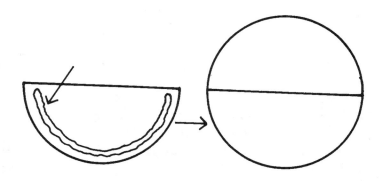

Directions:
1. Cut two 7 in. (18 cm) circles and eight 2 in. (5 cm) circles from craft foam.
2. Cut one 7 in. (18 cm) circle in half. Run a line of glue around the circular edge. Lining up the edges, glue the half circle onto the other 7 in. (18 cm) circle to create a pocket. This is the flower center.
3. Glue the ends of the 12 in. (30 cm) long piece of ribbon to the back of the pocket as a handle as shown. Let it dry.
4. Glue all of the smaller circles to the back of the flower center to form flower petals.
5. Glue two wiggle eyes above the pocket.
6. Using markers, draw a mouth on the pocket and decorate the petals.
7. Glue sequins to the blossom basket for additional decoration.
8. Fill the pocket with artificial or dried flowers or small treats.

Cinco de Mayo Piñata

Cinco de Mayo is an important Mexican holiday celebrated on May 5. It commemorates the Mexican Army's victory over a French army at the Battle of Puebla in 1862. Many parades and festivals are held to observe the holiday. Have the children make their own personal piñatas to use as they celebrate Cinco de Mayo.

Materials needed:
- donkey pattern on page 74
- tissue paper
- scissors
- glue
- card stock
- yarn
- crepe paper streamers or tissue paper
- 2 large wiggle eyes
- clothespins

Directions:
1. Reproduce two donkey patterns found on page 74 onto card stock and cut them out.
2. Glue the two donkey pieces together, leaving the back end of the shape open.
3. Cut strips of tissue paper or crepe paper about 2 in. (5 cm) in length. Cut multiple slits three-quarters of the way through each strip (width-wise).
4. Glue the strips lengthwise, each one overlapping the next, all the way along both sides of the donkey's body.
5. Punch a hole at the middle of the donkey's back.
6. Run a long piece of yarn through the hole and tie a knot to form a loop to serve as a hanger.
7. Cut two ears from tissue paper and glue them and the wiggle eyes, one on each side, to the donkey's head.
8. Stuff the donkey with pieces of candy. Glue a yarn tail at the back of the shape between the two pieces of card stock. Glue the opening shut, holding it closed with a clothespin until it is dry.

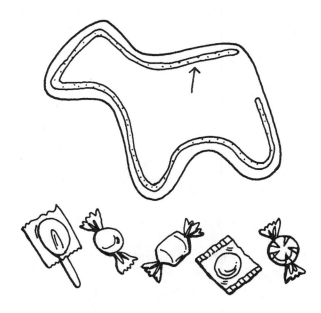

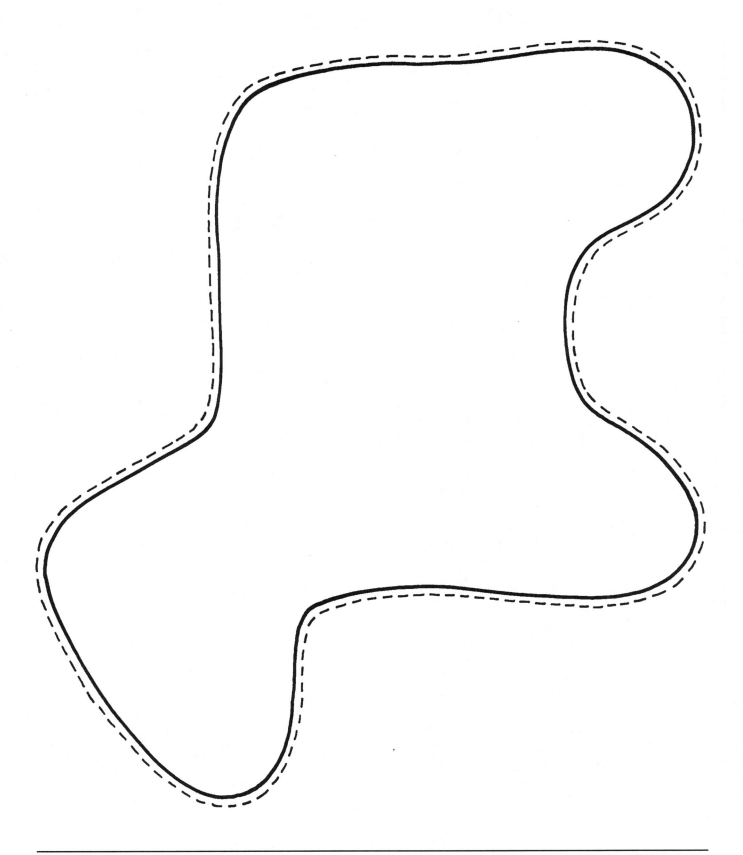

Mother's Day Hand Bouquet

Mothers love receiving cards and gifts from their children, especially handmade ones. This truly "handmade" gift combines two of a mom's favorites—their child's handprints and flowers—into one special gift for her. Children will enjoy tracing their own hands onto paper as they create bouquets for their moms.

Materials needed:
- pencil
- cupcake papers
- construction paper
- scissors
- glue
- chenille stems
- tissue paper
- pony beads
- decorations: sequins, glitter, or paper scraps

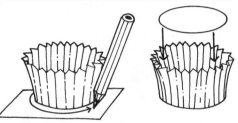

Directions:
1. Using a pencil, trace the child's hands onto folded construction paper, aligning the pinky fingers along the fold. Cut around the hands except on the fold.
2. Cut a circle the size of the bottom of the cupcake paper from construction paper.
3. Glue one end of a green chenille stem to the circle.
4. Glue the circle to the outside bottom of the cupcake paper, making sure to sandwich the chenille stem in between the layers.
5. Decorate the center of the cupcake paper flower with sequins, glitter, or paper scraps.
6. Cut the edge of the cupcake paper to form petals if desired.
7. Glue green paper leaves to the stem.
8. To make additional flowers, repeat steps 2–7.
9. Glue the chenille stem of each flower into the crease of the folded hands card.

Nature Walk Mobile

Celebrate the season by taking your students on a walk to help them become more aware of the wonders of nature. Supply small resealable plastic bags for the students to use while collecting natural treasures to take back to the classroom. Be sure they know which items of nature are appropriate to take and which should be left. While shells, sticks, nuts, acorns, fallen leaves, and seed pods are excellent materials, living plants or animals should be left for others to enjoy. Once you have returned to the classroom, have the children examine their collections and choose the best items to display on their mobiles.

Materials needed:
- tissue or paper towel cardboard tube
- jute, twine, or any natural-looking cord
- clean, dry sand
- glue
- scissors
- small natural items collected on the nature walk (twigs, leaves, shells, seeds, pods, stones, nuts)

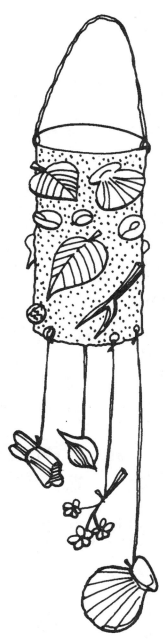

Directions:
1. Punch two holes evenly spaced at one end of the tube (for hanging later) and several holes evenly spaced around the other end.
2. Coat the outside of the tube with glue and roll it in clean dry sand. Let the glue dry.
3. Glue some of the natural items found on the walk to the sand-textured tube. Tie or glue the remaining objects onto strands of cord and attach them around the bottom of the mobile.
4. Tie each end of a long cord to the two holes at the top of the tube to serve as a hanger.

Fireworks Mobile

If your school is in session during summer, you can make this mobile to celebrate Independence Day. If not, use this craft activity to fill one of those last crazy days before summer vacation begins. The children can then take home this project and use it as a decoration when the Fourth of July rolls around.

Materials needed:
- ◉ small oatmeal box
- ◉ black glitter felt
- ◉ 14 in. (36 cm) piece of string
- ◉ glitter chenille stems
- ◉ craft wire
- ◉ glitter glue in assorted colors
  (or loose glitter and glue)
- ◉ glue
- ◉ scissors

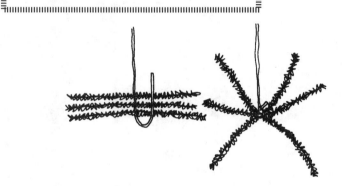

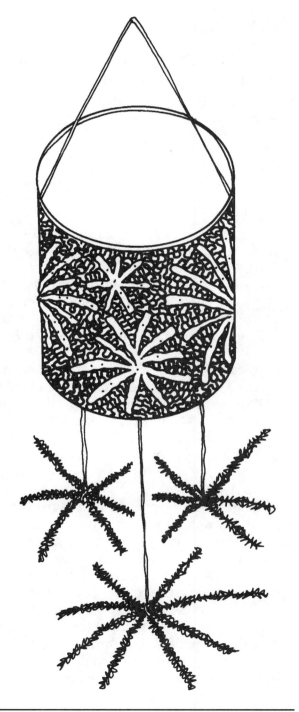

Directions:
1. Cover a circular oatmeal box with the black glitter felt.
2. Draw fireworks bursts onto the felt with glitter glue, or with glue sprinkled with loose glitter, and let them dry.
3. Make fireworks by bundling several pieces of glittery chenille stems together and securing them with wire in the center.
4. Bend the chenille stems to form firework shapes.
5. Tie the chenille stem fireworks to strings and attach them around the bottom of the oatmeal box.
6. Punch two holes in the top of the oatmeal box and tie the 14 in. (36 cm) long string to both holes to serve as a hanger.

Peat Cup Birdhouses

Birdhouses are no longer just outdoor objects. The popularity of the birdhouse as home decor has grown considerably in recent years. Children will be proud to take these adorable birdhouses home to display.

Materials needed:
- ⊚ pencil
- ⊚ 12 in. (30 cm) piece of yarn or ribbon
- ⊚ birdhouse roof pattern
- ⊚ peat cups
- ⊚ glue
- ⊚ Spanish moss
- ⊚ dried or artificial flowers
- ⊚ chenille stem

Directions:

1. Using a pencil, poke a full-size hole in the lower part of the peat cup for the entrance to the birdhouse. Just below the entrance, poke a small hole with the tip of the pencil and glue a chenille stem in the hole for the perch.

2. Fold a 12 in. (30 cm) length of yarn in half and tie two knots on top of each other to form a loop.

3. Measure the diameter at the top of the peat cup. Divide the measurement in half and then add an additional inch. (Example: if an opening is 2 in. (5 cm) in diameter, then you add 1 in. (25 mm).

4. Cut a circle with a diameter of 3 in. (7 cm) and mark a dot in the very center of the circle.

5. Using scissors, cut from the outside to the center dot. Slide the yarn loop through the slit up to the center of the circle and add a dab of glue to hold it in place.

6. With the loop extending from the top, overlap one flap of the circle over the other to form a cone that will fit over the top of the peat cup. Glue or staple the flaps together.

7. Add a line of glue around the top of the peat cup and glue the roof to the top.

8. Decorate the birdhouse with moss, flowers, and ribbon as desired.

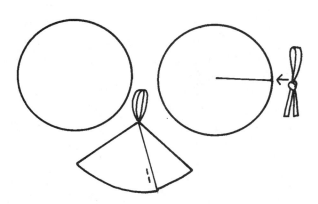

My Circus

Going to the circus is exciting, and creating a circus of your own can be as well. Children will have a great time making these circus characters and playing with them as finger puppets. The puppets will store nicely in the lunch bag Circus Cage that the children will also make.

Circus Cage
Materials needed:
- pattern on page 82
- 1 brown lunch sack
- white card stock
- markers or crayons
- 3 craft sticks
- glitter, sequins, and acrylic rhinestones
- pencil
- scissors
- glue

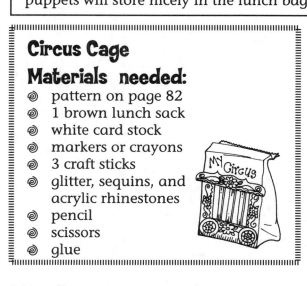

Directions:
1. Reproduce the cage pattern (page 82) onto white card stock, color, and cut out.
2. Lay the cage at the base of the sack as shown and trace around the inside of the window with your pencil. Cut out the window shape you have drawn on the sack.
3. Glue three craft sticks evenly apart to the back of the cage window and let dry.
4. Line the base of the cage with the bottom edge of the sack and glue it in place.
5. Complete by decorating the cage with markers or crayons, glitter glue, sequins, and acrylic rhinestones.

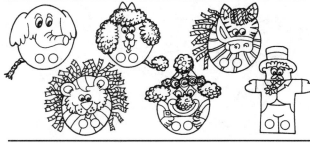

Finger People and Animals
Materials needed:
- puppets patterns on pages 80–82
- white card stock
- markers or crayons
- glitter, sequins, acrylic rhinestones
- pencil
- scissors
- glue

Finger People and Animals
Directions:
1. Reproduce patterns onto white card stock.
2. Color with markers and cut out. Decorate as desired (see tips below).

Performer: add a feather to the hat, sequins to the dress, and eyes to the face

Circus man: add sequins to flower, eyes to face

Elephant: add a string tail

Lion: add wiggle eyes and yarn hair for the mane

Poodle: add wiggle eyes and a little pink pom-pom nose to the face, cotton ball ears to the head, short yarn tail with cotton ball glued on the end to the body

Horse: add a feather on top of the head, wiggle eyes to face, yarn mane to body, and sequins to harness

Clown: add wiggle eyes, big red pom-pom nose to face, pom-pom to top of hat, yarn hair to head, and crumpled tissue to hat brim

Bear: add a brown pom-pom nose to face

Tiger: add wiggle eyes to face, glue on stripes from black and orange chenille stems or yarn

Zebra: add wiggle eyes, glue on stripes from black chenille stems or yarn

Popcorn: glue cotton swab tips onto the bag

Cotton candy: tint a cotton ball with pink or blue marker and glue it on

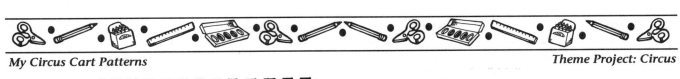

Circus Cat Photo Frames

After creating your circus, make these circus cat photo frames that the children can bring home to their parents. Before starting this craft, take a picture of each child holding the characters completed in "My Circus." Then let each child choose a favorite big cat (leopard, tiger, lion, etc.) and use the pattern to include it on their circus cat photo frame.

Materials needed:
- ◎ cat patterns below
- ◎ 8 wooden craft sticks (plain or colored)
- ◎ craft foam
- ◎ wiggle eyes
- ◎ glue
- ◎ yarn
- ◎ black permanent marker
- ◎ waxed paper

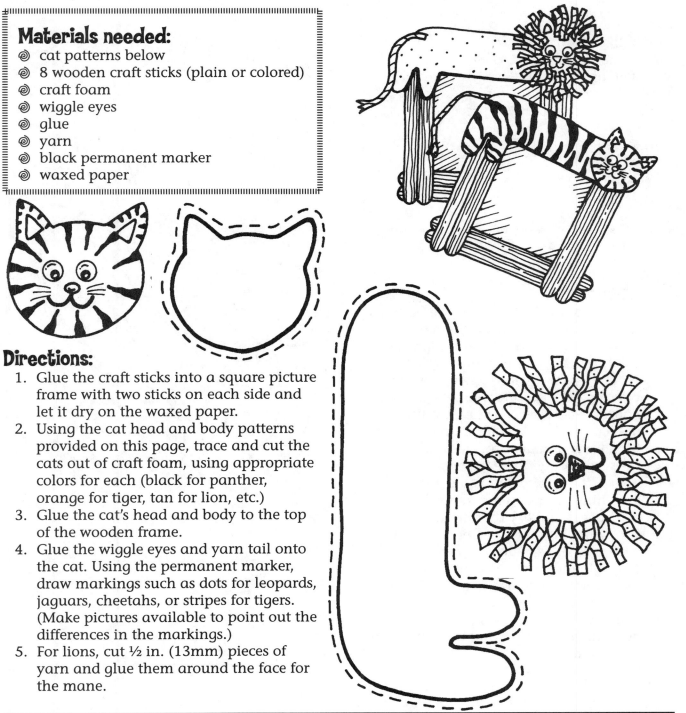

Directions:
1. Glue the craft sticks into a square picture frame with two sticks on each side and let it dry on the waxed paper.
2. Using the cat head and body patterns provided on this page, trace and cut the cats out of craft foam, using appropriate colors for each (black for panther, orange for tiger, tan for lion, etc.)
3. Glue the cat's head and body to the top of the wooden frame.
4. Glue the wiggle eyes and yarn tail onto the cat. Using the permanent marker, draw markings such as dots for leopards, jaguars, cheetahs, or stripes for tigers. (Make pictures available to point out the differences in the markings.)
5. For lions, cut ½ in. (13mm) pieces of yarn and glue them around the face for the mane.

Fun Fruit and Veggies

Are there children in your class that are having trouble learning or keeping the colors straight? This is where *Fun Fruit and Veggies* can be used as an instructional tool. This simple craft can be used for color recognition while teaching a unit on fruits and vegetables.

Materials needed:
- ◉ patterns on pages 85–88
- ◉ felt: green, light green, red, orange, tan, purple, white, and yellow
- ◉ purple craft foam (or precut purple circles)
- ◉ glue
- ◉ marker
- ◉ scissors
- ◉ fiberfill
- ◉ clothespins

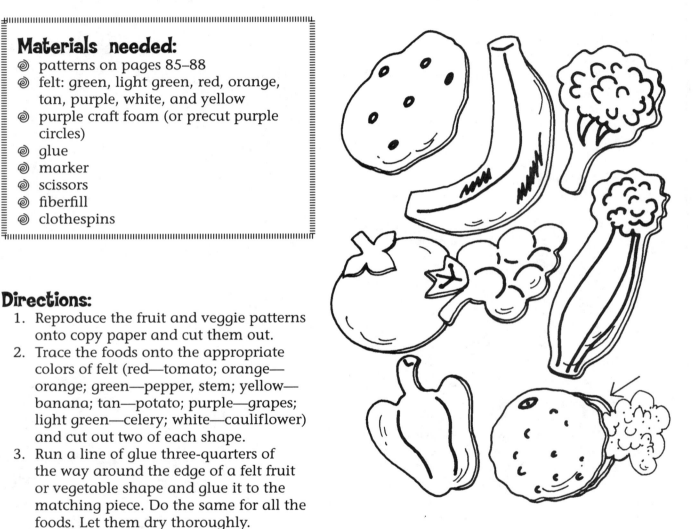

Directions:
1. Reproduce the fruit and veggie patterns onto copy paper and cut them out.
2. Trace the foods onto the appropriate colors of felt (red—tomato; orange—orange; green—pepper, stem; yellow—banana; tan—potato; purple—grapes; light green—celery; white—cauliflower) and cut out two of each shape.
3. Run a line of glue three-quarters of the way around the edge of a felt fruit or vegetable shape and glue it to the matching piece. Do the same for all the foods. Let them dry thoroughly.
4. Use a small amount of fiberfill to stuff each fruit or vegetable.
5. Then glue the open edge of each filled food shape closed. Hold it closed with clothespins until thoroughly dry.
7. Remove the clothespins and add detail patterns to the fruits and vegetables with a black marker.

Tip:
A plastic ice-cream container makes a great place for each child to store the fruits and vegetables.

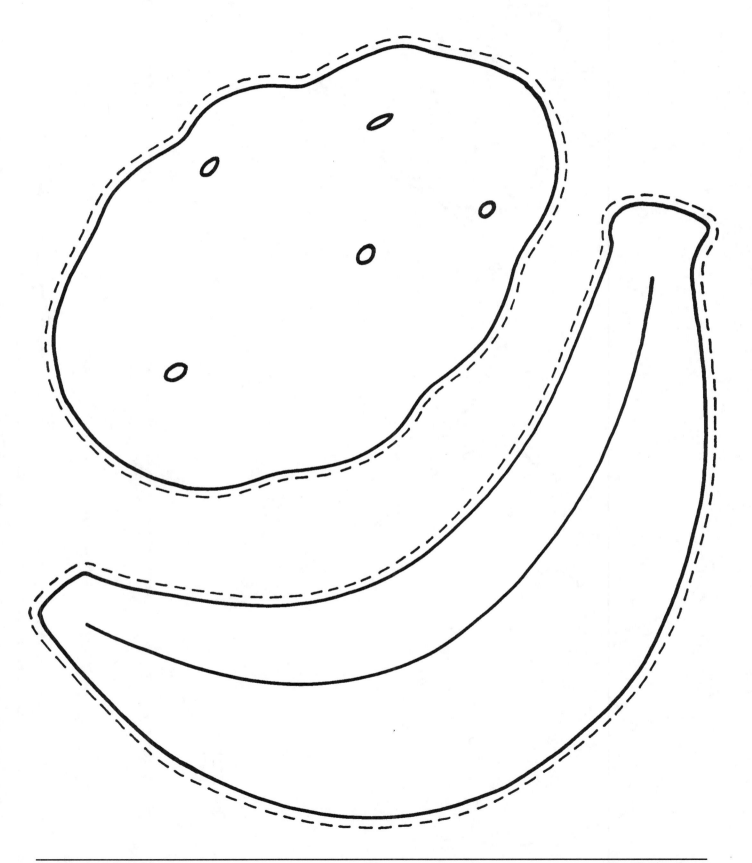

Community Helpers

No early childhood curriculum would be complete without a unit on community helpers. Teaching children about those people that serve us is a very worthwhile lesson. While playing with the community helper figures and clothing provided on the following pages, the children can be learning valuable information about the careers of those people in their community.

Materials needed:
- ✺ patterns found on pages 90–94
- ✺ white card stock
- ✺ crayons or markers
- ✺ restickable glue stick
- ✺ scissors

Directions:
1. Reproduce the community helper paper dolls and clothing patterns onto white card stock.
2. Color the paper dolls and community helpers' clothing and cut them out.
3. Apply one or two strokes of restickable glue to the back of the clothing patterns before dressing the community helpers.

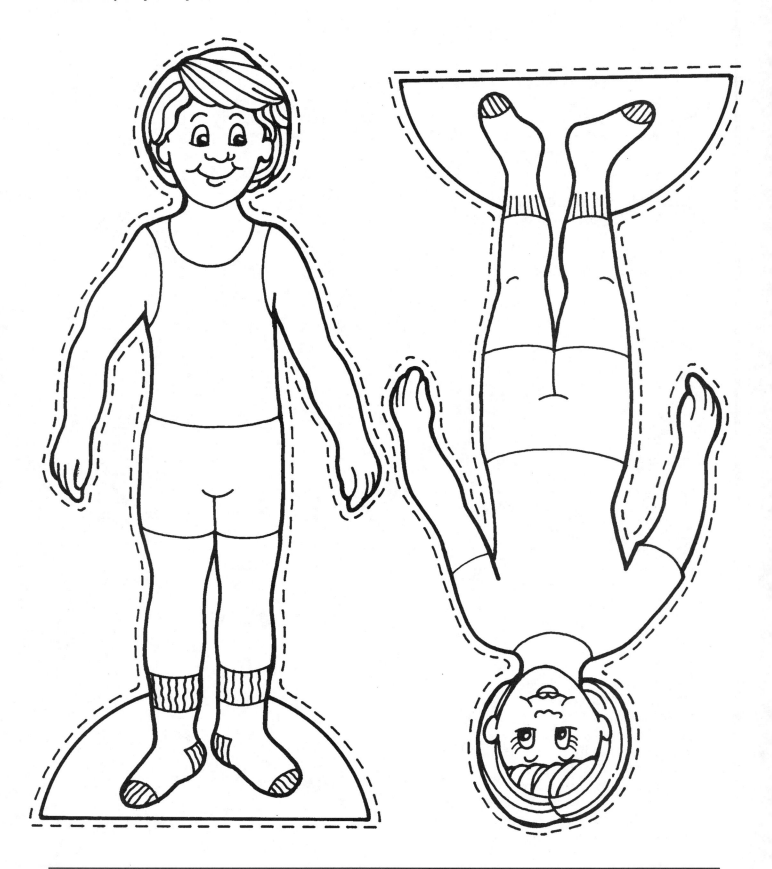

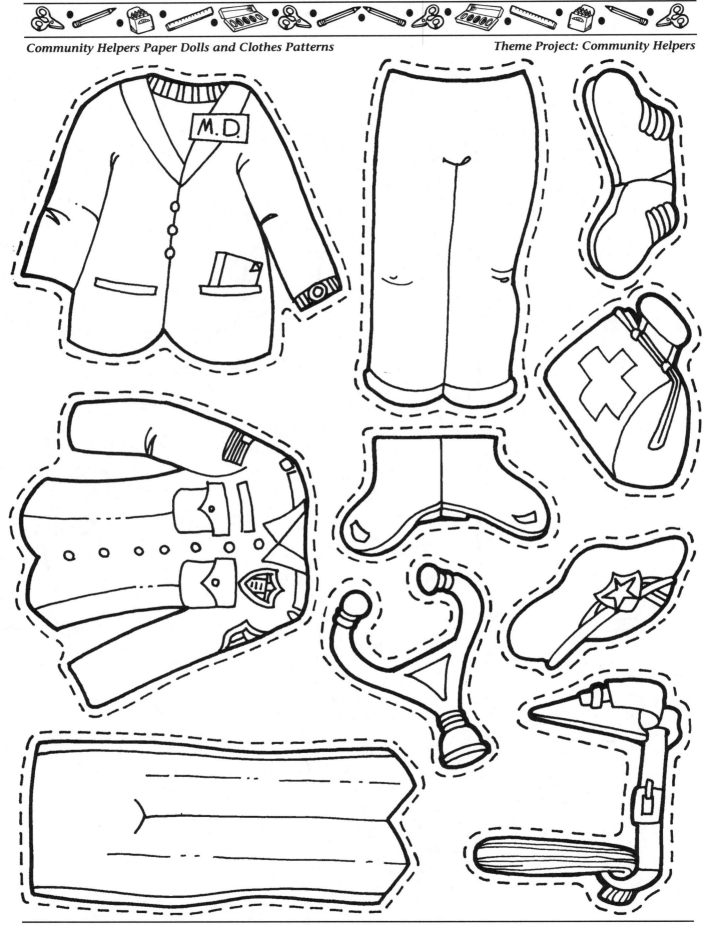

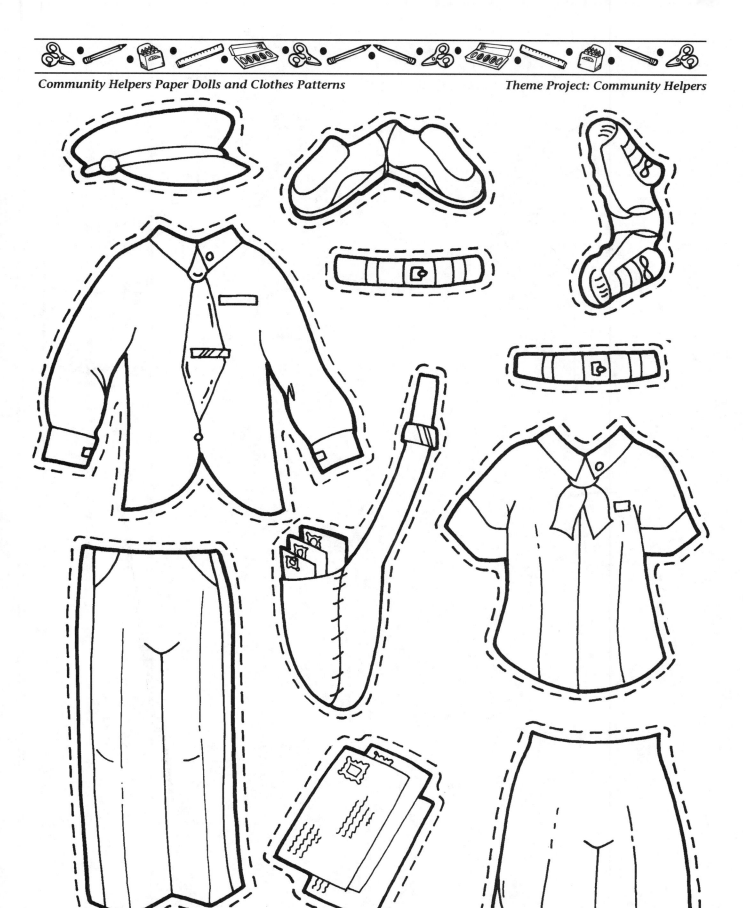

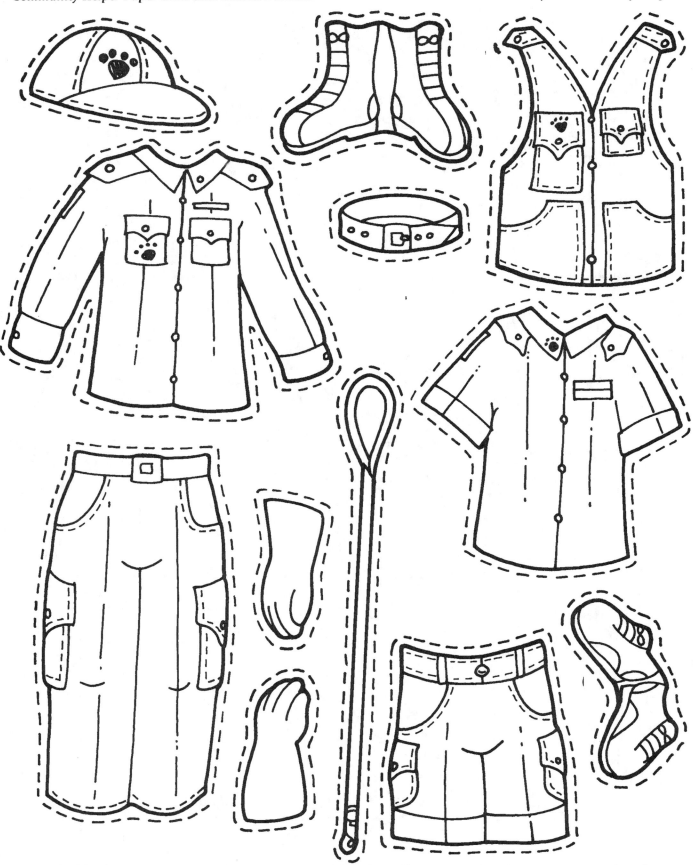

Community Vehicles

Every community helper needs a vehicle for transportation. Who could imagine a firefighter without a fire truck or an EMT without an ambulance? Making vehicles for the community helpers that you created (see page 89) can be easily constructed by using an assortment of product boxes along with all of the vehicle accessory patterns included on the following pages.

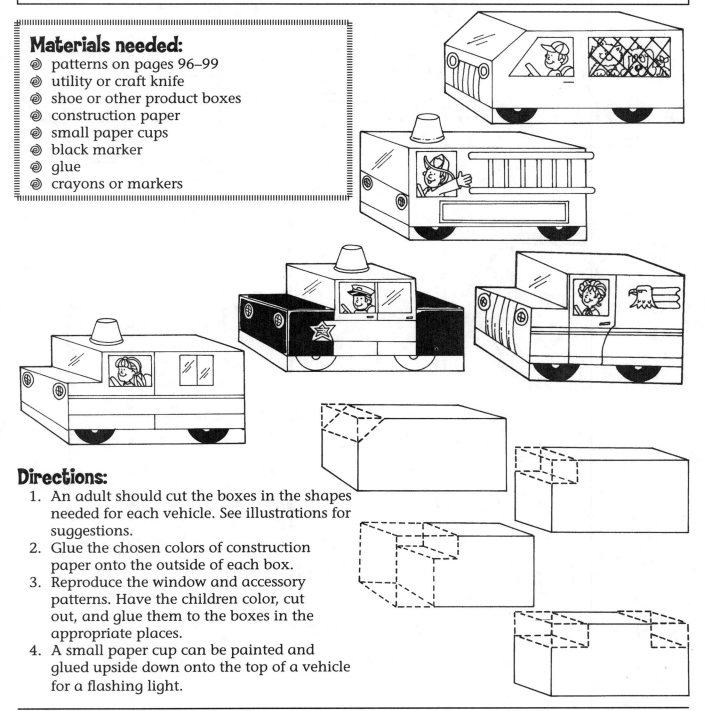

Materials needed:
- patterns on pages 96–99
- utility or craft knife
- shoe or other product boxes
- construction paper
- small paper cups
- black marker
- glue
- crayons or markers

Directions:
1. An adult should cut the boxes in the shapes needed for each vehicle. See illustrations for suggestions.
2. Glue the chosen colors of construction paper onto the outside of each box.
3. Reproduce the window and accessory patterns. Have the children color, cut out, and glue them to the boxes in the appropriate places.
4. A small paper cup can be painted and glued upside down onto the top of a vehicle for a flashing light.

97

My Dinosaur Book

Whether it is the dinosaur's enormous size or its unique features—children are fascinated with dinosaurs! They can identify them by shape and many times even pronounce their enormous names! The construction of this booklet allows children to carry their dinosaurs along wherever they go.

Materials needed:

- ◎ dinosaur patterns on pages 101–103
- ◎ assorted colors of construction paper
- ◎ white card stock
- ◎ scissors
- ◎ pencil
- ◎ crayons or markers
- ◎ paper punch
- ◎ glue
- ◎ yarn or staples for binding
- ◎ decorative items (artificial leaves and flowers, cotton batting, sandpaper, felt, textured fabric scraps, or lightweight vinyls, and upholstery scraps)

Directions:

1. Reproduce the dinosaur patterns onto white card stock, reducing or enlarging them as needed.
2. Create a simple book cover and book pages by cutting construction paper sheets in half, or get creative and cut the cover and pages into matching dinosaur egg or bone shapes.
3. Lightly draw your title in pencil on the cover. Then trace with marker. Finish the cover by decorating it with drawings, cutouts, or artificial flowers to create a tropical look. *(Suggestions: add dinosaur footprints, palm trees, flowers, a forest, or dinosaur heads.)*
4. Color the dinosaur shapes that have been reproduced onto white card stock or use them as patterns and cut the shapes from construction paper, interesting designed or textured fabric, or sandpaper.
5. Glue a dinosaur to each book page and create a background. Older children may wish to write something about each dinosaur on the page.

Extra suggestions:

- Use batting to create clouds.
- Sandpaper can be used for dinosaur skin, tree trunks, and stones. Try coloring the sandpaper with crayons for a very different textured look.
- Glue artificial leaves to the tops of trees or in clusters to create shrubs.
- Cut dinosaur shapes from patterned felt, or by using a variety of textured and patterned fabrics, such as velvet, vinyls, or upholstery scraps for a snakeskin look.

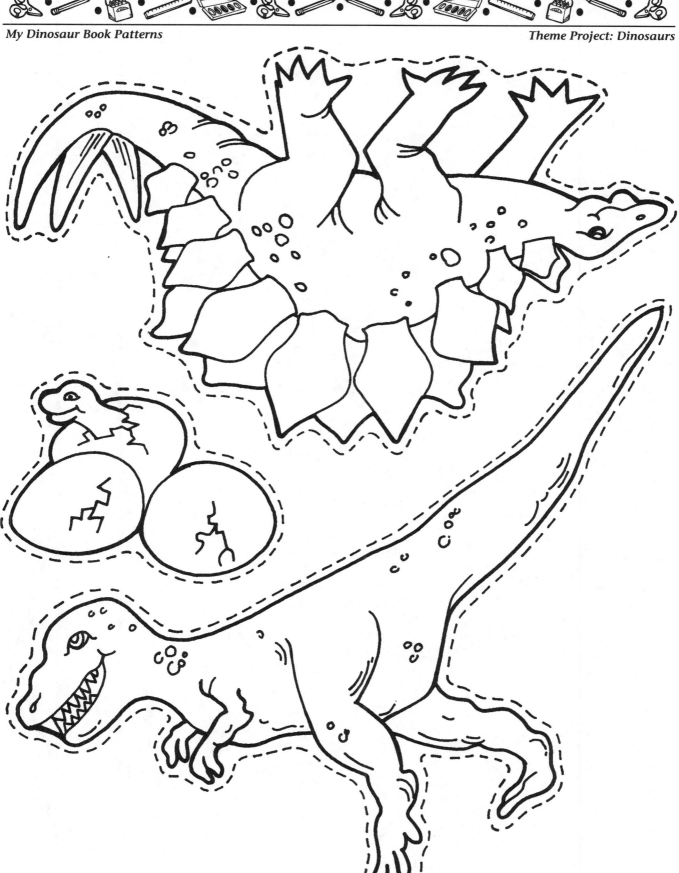

My Farm

For children who live on farms or visit farms often, this craft will be a familiar lesson. For those children who are unfamiliar with farms, it will be an enjoyable learning experience. Most children have a fascination with animals, so creating farm animals of their own to play with should prove to be a lot of fun!

The Barn

Materials needed:
- cardboard box
- cardboard sheets (roof)
- craft knife
- pencil
- ruler
- red, white, and green paint
- paintbrush
- water container
- paper towels
- newspapers
- glue
- masking tape

Directions:
1. Using a pencil, draw a roof line along the top of the box. Have an adult cut along the line with the craft knife.
2. Draw a barn door and cut along the top of the door and down the center to make double doors that open.
3. Draw and cut out windows on the barn.
4. Measure the roofline and cut a cardboard rectangle for the roof that is 2 in. (5 cm) larger than the length and the width. Fold the rectangle in half.
5. Cover the work area with newspaper. Paint the barn red. After the paint dries, add the trim around the barn door and windows. Paint a big "X" on the barn doors.
6. Paint the roof green.
7. Run a thick line of glue around the roofline. Carefully place the roof on the barn. If needed, reinforce the roof by taping strips of masking tape that connect the underside of the roof to the barn.

Farm Animals, Tractor, and Farmer

Materials needed:
- patterns found on pages 105–107
- white card
- scissors
- crayons or markers

Directions:
1. Reproduce the patterns onto card stock.
2. Cut out the shapes.
3. Color with crayons or markers.
4. Assemble them onto stands as shown on page 107.

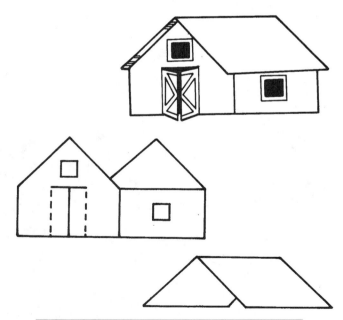

Tip:
Enlist parents or volunteers to help with the cutting of the boxes.

My Farm Patterns

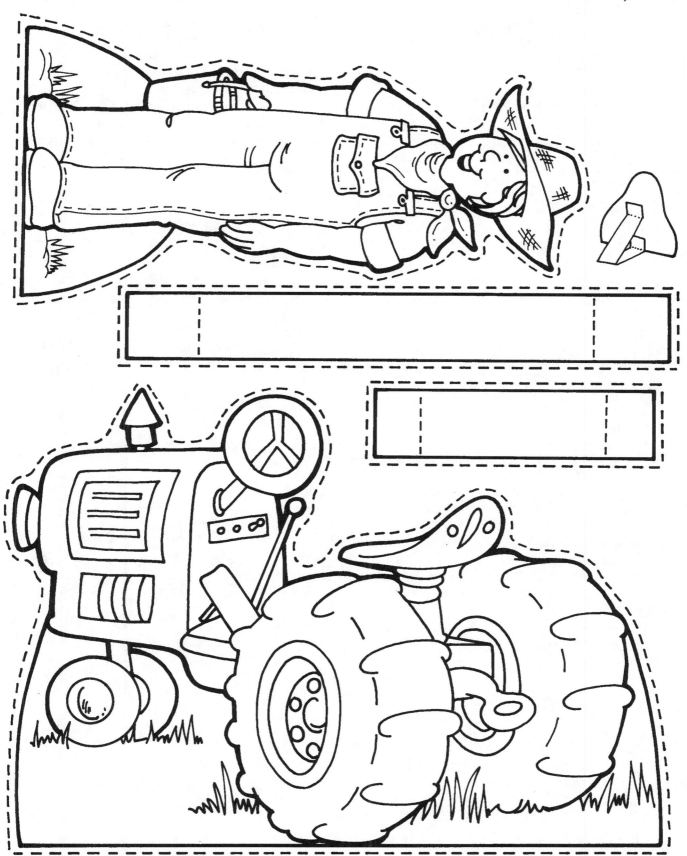

Helping Hands Coupon Book

Does your class celebrate Grandparents' Day at school? Are you searching for a clever gift idea for grandparents? Look no further. Grandparents will adore the books made with their grandchildren's hands. Each book is full of coupons that grant them special activities with their grandchild. Encourage the children to fill their books with activities that do not require money, such as a hug, doing dishes, sweeping the driveway or garage, or baking cookies—things that grandchildren and grandparents can do together.

Materials needed:
- craft foam
- 9 in. x 12 in. (23 cm x 30 cm) construction paper
- black permanent marker
- paper punch
- twine or yarn
- pencil
- scissors

Directions:
1. Trace the child's hand on craft foam and cut it out.
2. Booklet options according to cutting ability:
   Booklet Option A: Fold two or three sheets of construction paper together. Trace the child's hand on the construction paper and cut through as many sheets as possible at once, making four to six hand-shaped pages. (Younger children may need help with the cutting.)
   Booklet Option B: For less cutting, cut a sheet of construction paper in half. Then fold that sheet in half and glue the craft foam hand to it to create the cover. Make pages by cutting and folding construction paper as done for the cover.
3. Write "Helping Hands" on the craft foam hand with a black permanent marker.
4. Write "To: _____
        From: _____," on the first page. Write "Good for _____" on all of the other pages and have each child fill in the blanks.
5. ***Option 1:*** Punch a hole at the bottom of the craft foam hand and tie twine through it.
6. ***Option 2:*** Punch two holes along the left edge of the completed book and tie twine or yarn through them.
7. Encourage the children to draw hearts, XXX's and OOO's, or "I love you's" on the booklet.

Tip:
If you have willing adult volunteers, have them help cut out the paper and craft foam hand shapes.

Family Tree

Creating a family tree can make a special gift for any family member. This is also a fun activity for helping the children get to know the other children in class through learning about each other's families. This activity is also easy to make.

Materials needed:
- green poster board
- toilet paper tube
- pencil
- compass
- markers or crayons
- green construction paper
- scissors
- decorative-edged scissors
- glue
- pencil

Directions:
1. Using a compass, draw a 4 in. (10 cm) circle and a 7 in. (18 cm) circle on green poster board. Cut the circles out with decorative edged scissors. If green poster board is not available, glue green construction paper to white poster board before drawing the circles.
2. Color a toilet paper tube to look like tree bark using brown and tan markers or crayons.
3. Cut two 1½ in. (38 mm) long slits directly across from each other on one end of the toilet paper tube.
4. Run a thick line of glue around the other end of the tube and glue it to the center of the smaller green circle. Let it dry.
5. While the base dries, begin drawing your family tree branches on the 7" (18 cm) treetop circle. Begin by lightly drawing the branches on the treetop using a pencil and then color them with markers or crayons. Cut out leaves from green construction paper. Write your family names on the leaves and glue them to the appropriate branches. When finished, slide the treetop circle into the slits on the tree trunk.

Handy Clips

These handy clothespin-clip refrigerator magnets are not only cute but are useful. Their placement on the refrigerator gives easy access to the clips that can be used to hold recipes and other special items. These refrigerator magnets will also make nice gifts for relatives and friends.

Materials needed:
- poster board
- yellow felt
- compass
- glue
- 2 wiggle eyes
- black permanent marker
- 6–8 small clothespins
- magnetic strips

Directions:
1. Using a compass, draw a 4 in. (10 cm) circle on poster board and cut it out.
2. Trace the poster board circle onto yellow felt.
3. Cut out the yellow felt circle and glue it on the poster board circle.
4. Draw a smiling mouth on the yellow felt. Glue on two wiggle eyes above the mouth.
5. Paint the clothespins yellow and let dry.
6. Glue a magnetic strip to the back of each clothespin and to the back of the poster board circle.
7. Once the clothespins have dried, clip them around the edges of the yellow circle to create a smiling sun.

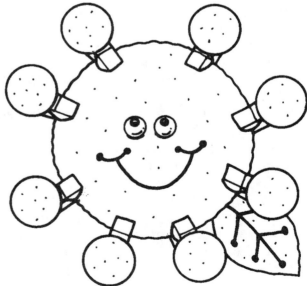

Tip:
Create a flower clip by following the directions above. Then add 1 in. (25 mm) circles cut from pastel-colored felt. Glue a circle to each clothespin handle to create a flower petal.

Mosaic Key Holder

Here is a great Father's Day gift idea! This key holder can be made from a variety of materials, such as mosaic pieces, beans, rice, pasta, or simple craft foam scraps that have been cut into small pieces.

Materials needed:
- one 5 in. x 7 in. (13 cm x 18 cm) wooden picture frame with hanger
- 5 in. x 7 in. (13 cm x 18 cm) stiff cardboard
- 3 cup hooks
- acrylic paint
- pencil
- glue
- paintbrush
- mosaic pieces: a variety of dried beans, rice, pasta, fun foam cut into small pieces, or packaged mosaic pieces

Directions:
1. In advance, screw three cup hooks evenly spaced across the bottom of the frame. It may be necessary to predrill small starter holes before attaching the cup hooks.
2. Choose a background color for your mosaic and paint the 5" x 7" (13 cm x 17 cm) cardboard that color. Let it dry.
3. Run a line of glue along the outer edge of the cardboard and insert it into the frame.
4. Lightly draw a simple picture on the painted cardboard.
5. Choose the appropriate color mosaic pieces for the picture. Using your drawing as a guide, glue the mosaic materials to the painted board, leaving a small space between each mosaic piece so that the background color shows. Let the glue dry.

Zany Pencil Holder

Looking for an interesting new way to keep pencils from rolling away? Or perhaps you need a clever idea for a Christmas, Hanukkah, or Father's Day gift? Children will have a "nutty" time while creating this clay pencil holder.

Materials needed:
- ◎ oven bake modeling clay
- ◎ pencil
- ◎ assortment of screws, bolts, nails, washers, and nuts
- ◎ 4 in. (10 cm) square of aluminum foil
- ◎ baking sheet
- ◎ oven

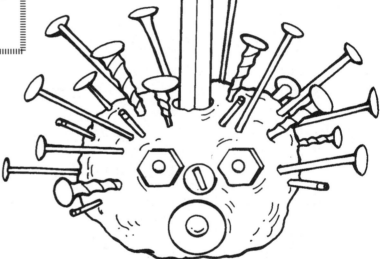

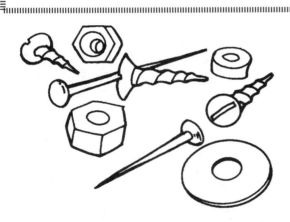

Directions:

1. Knead a ball of clay about the size of a small plum until it is soft and easy to shape. Form the clay into any shape desired and firmly place it on the foil sheet so it stands steady.

2. Insert the pencil halfway into the top of the shape to form the holder.

3. Leaving the pencil in the clay, create a zany face on the clay shape by pressing an assortment of hardware into the clay.

4. After the pencil holder is decorated, gently wiggle the pencil back and forth to remove it from the clay. Place the pencil holder and the foil onto a cookie sheet and bake as directed by the clay manufacturer's instructions.

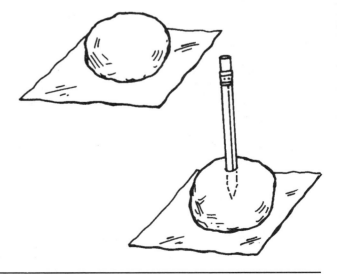

Frog Paperweight

Frogs are one of the most fascinating creatures, and in spring and summer they literally start "popping up" everywhere. As children create their own fun frogs from smooth stones, they are also making useful paperweights which can be given as gifts.

Materials needed:
- smooth stones (found in craft stores)
- dark green, light green, yellow, and orange paint
- green craft foam
- colored markers
- wiggle eyes
- red ribbon
- tacky glue
- white or pink artificial flower with the stem removed
- scissors
- paintbrushes
- water
- containers
- paper towels
- newspapers to cover work area

Directions:
1. To make a lily pad, cut out your own design from craft foam or use the pattern provided.
2. Choose one or two small stones for the frogs and paint them light or dark green. Use the other green, yellow, or orange paint to create spots on the backs of the frogs. Let them dry.
3. Paint or draw a small mouth on the front of each frog as shown.
4. Cut out a small piece of ribbon and glue it to the frog's mouth to create a tongue.
5. Glue on two wiggle eyes. Glue the frog to the lily pad.
6. To finish, glue the artificial flower to the lily pad.

Egg Carton Creatures

Creepy, crawly organisms are intriguing and can enthrall children for hours. Give your students a hands-on project with these egg carton creatures. They are easy to make and fun to play with.

Materials needed:
- cardboard egg cartons
- black, red, orange, yellow, and green paint
- paintbrush
- green and brown chenille stems
- wiggle eyes
- glue
- clear sheets of acetate
- raffia
- small black pom-pom
- black pony bead
- black permanent marker

For all insects mentioned, except the grasshopper, cut one egg-holder cup from a cardboard egg carton and cut the rough edge off flat so it will sit evenly. Cut out two connected egg-holder cups for the grasshopper.

Ladybug Directions:
1. Paint the front of the egg-holder cup black and the back red. Let it dry. Draw a line down the center of the red back and add dots with a black permanent marker.
2. Glue a small black pom-pom onto the upper front of the body and glue two wiggle eyes on the pom-pom.
3. Poke three 2 in. (5 cm) long chenille legs through each side of the ladybug's body near the bottom and fold them over on the under side.

Snail Directions:

1. Paint the egg-holder cup yellow. Let it dry.
2. Coil two brown chenille stems in tight spirals. Glue one spiral to each side of the egg-holder cup.
3. Glue two 2 in. (5 cm) pieces of unfolded raffia together. Let it dry. Cut a slit (an adult should do this) at the bottom front of the snail body and insert the raffia neck. Glue it in place.
4. To create the antennae, twist a yellow chenille stem around the raffia.

Bumblebee Directions:
1. Alternate paint stripes of black and yellow on the egg-holder cup. Let it dry.
2. Glue a black pony bead to the upper front. Glue two wiggle eyes onto the pony bead.
3. Cut out teardrop shape wings from an acetate sheet. Draw veins on the wings with a permanent marker. Cut slits near the top in both sides of the egg-holder cup to insert the wings. Add a dab of glue to each wing to hold it in place. (A fly can be made the same way by painting the egg-holder cup black.)

Grasshopper Directions:

1. Paint the two egg-holder cups green.
2. Glue wiggle eyes near the top of one of the sides of the egg-holder cups.
3. Fashion legs from green chenille stems as shown. Then poke the legs through the sides of the egg-holder cups near the bottom and fold them over on the under side.

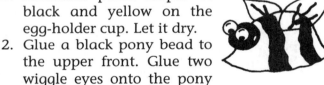

Theme Project: Learning Games

Classroom Mailboxes

What's more fun than getting mail? Let each child personalize a mailbox. The mailboxes could be decorated for Valentine's Day, in a patriotic fashion, or changed seasonally and used for special notes and birthday greetings.

Materials needed:
- cereal box
- scissors
- utility knife
  (for the teacher to cut a mail slot)
- glue
- construction paper
- felt and fabric scraps,
  decorative scrapbook
  papers, old lace trim,
  glitter glue, and stickers
- markers and crayons

Directions:
1. Cut off the box top as shown in drawing.
2. Trace front and side panels for the box onto construction paper. Cut out the shapes and glue them to the cereal box. (An adult should assist in cutting out the mail slots.)
3. Have the children decorate their mailboxes as desired, or as instructed if a theme is being used. Have the children print their names on the front of their mailboxes.
4. Reproduce postcard and stamp patterns (page 116) onto sheets of card stock and place them near the mailboxes so they are available for the children to use at any time.
5. Have the children color the stamps with crayons or fine-tip markers. Some children may prefer to design their own stamps on the materials provided.
6. Cut the postcards and stamps out along the dashed lines. Glue a stamp to the postcard.
7. Draw a picture or write a message on the postcards before "mailing" the greetings.

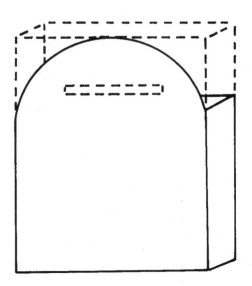

From: _____

_____

_____

To: _____

_____

_____

Gone Fishing Game

This *Gone Fishing Game* presents challenges to children in various ways. One challenge is for them to concentrate long enough to catch a fish using their magnetic fish hooks. The second challenge comes in learning something new when they are playing one of the educational games provided below.

Materials needed:
- patterns on pages 118-120
- dowel rods
- string
- small magnet (not magnetic strip)
- paper clips
- scissors
- paper punch
- glue
- construction paper or colored card stock
- decorative items: felt, craft foam, scraps, sequins, and glitter glue

Directions:
1. Tie a 12 in. (30 cm) string to one end of the dowel rod to make the fishing pole.
2. Using the pattern provided, cut out two matching fish hooks. Attach a magnet to the bottom of one of the fish hook shapes. Glue the other hook shape on top, sandwiching the magnet between the two hooks. Punch a hole at the top of the fishhook and tie it to the end of the fishing line. Decorate the hook if desired.
3. Reproduce the fish patterns onto colored card stock paper and cut them out or use the pattern shapes as a guide to cut out construction paper fish shapes.
4. Decorate each side of the fish shapes as desired with the items suggested above. Let the glue dry.
5. Attach a paperclip to the mouths of each fish.

Games Ideas:
1. Write numbers on the backs of the fish. Catch two fish and then add or subtract the numbers displayed on them. To increase the difficulty, catch and add together more than two numbers.
2. Write letters on the backs of the fish. Say a word that begins with the letter shown on the fish caught.
3. Write numbers on the backs of the fish and zeros on the hat, boot, snake, branch, etc. Divide the class into two teams. Blindfold the fishermen with fish-face masks (page 120). After everyone has had a turn fishing, have the children add up the points on the backs of what they caught to see which team earned the most points.

Fish-Face Mask Directions:
Decorate at least two masks—one for each team or have each child make their own mask.
1. Reproduce the fish-face mask pattern (page 120) onto card stock paper. Cut out the mask and decorate it as desired.
2. Tie a string or elastic cord through the holes indicated on the mask.

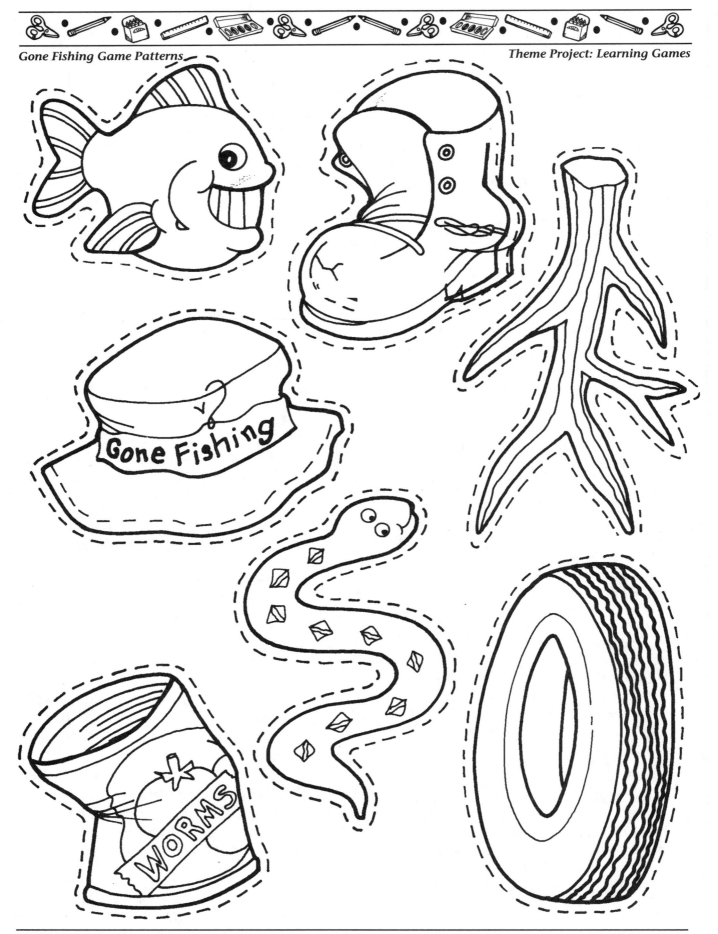

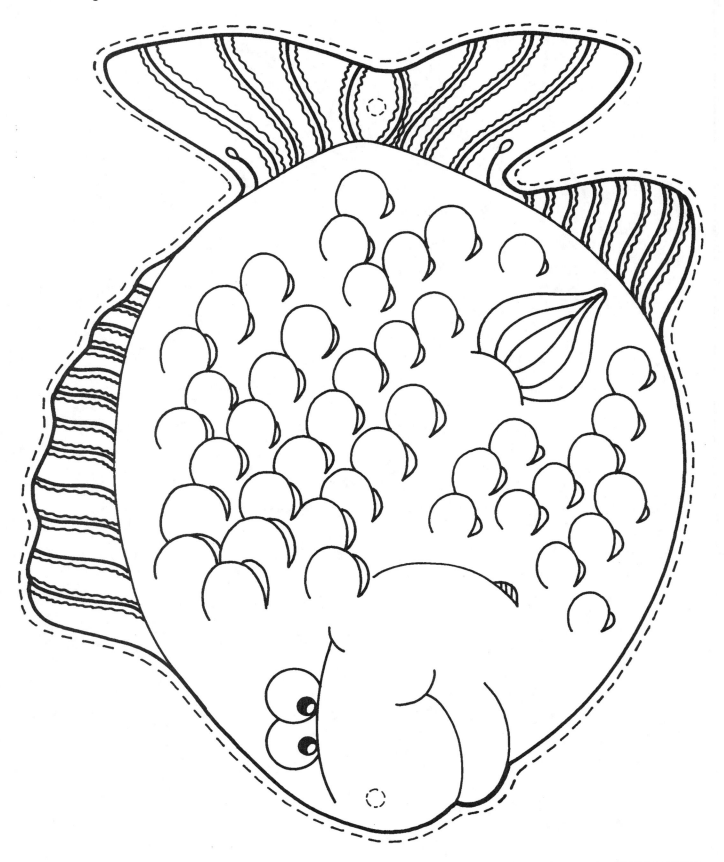

Teddy Bear Flash Card Holder

How excited children are when they first start to work with their flash cards! It is important that each child has a personalized set to use whenever free time arises. Use of this clever teddy bear holder will inspire each child to take home a set of flash cards for extra practice time.

Materials needed:
- ⚙ pattern on page 122
- ⚙ brown, tan, and pink felt
- ⚙ 2 wiggle eyes
- ⚙ 1 small black pom-pom
- ⚙ paper punch
- ⚙ ribbon or small shoelace
- ⚙ quilt batting
- ⚙ glue
- ⚙ scissors
- ⚙ black marker
- ⚙ waxed paper
- ⚙ heavy book
- ⚙ card stock

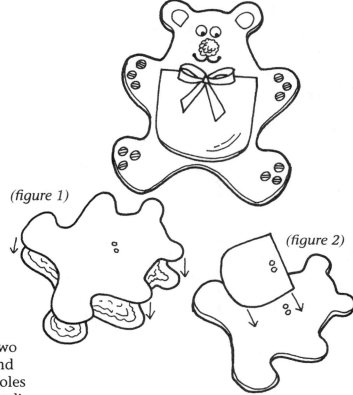

(figure 1)

(figure 2)

Directions:
1. Use the pattern provided and cut out two brown body shapes, one tan pocket, and two pink ears made from felt. Punch holes on one body shape and the pocket as indicated on the patterns.
2. Cut out the stuffing shape from quilt batting using the body-shaped pattern provided.
3. Run a line of glue just along the inside edge of the brown body shape that does not have holes. Lay the batting on the center of the bear body, then run another line of glue on the edge of the batting and place the other body shape on top, matching up the edges. (See figure 1.)
4. Lay the bear between a sandwich of waxed paper (to protect surfaces as it dries) and place a heavy book on top.
5. When the glue is dry, string an 8 in. (20 cm) long ribbon or small shoelace through the two holes on the body.

6. Run a line of glue around the sides and bottom edge of the pocket. Position the pocket on the bear's belly (glue side down), lining up the pocket punched holes over the holes on the bear body. (See figure 2.)
7. Glue the ears, eyes, and pom-pom nose onto the bear. Use a black marker to draw the mouth and paw marks.
8. Reproduce the flash card patterns (page 123) onto card stock. (Fill out the flash cards before reproducing them, or let the children fill out the blank cards.) Provide each child with sheets of flash cards to cut out and place in the bear's pocket.
9. String the ribbon ends through the holes in the pocket and tie closed until ready to use the cards.

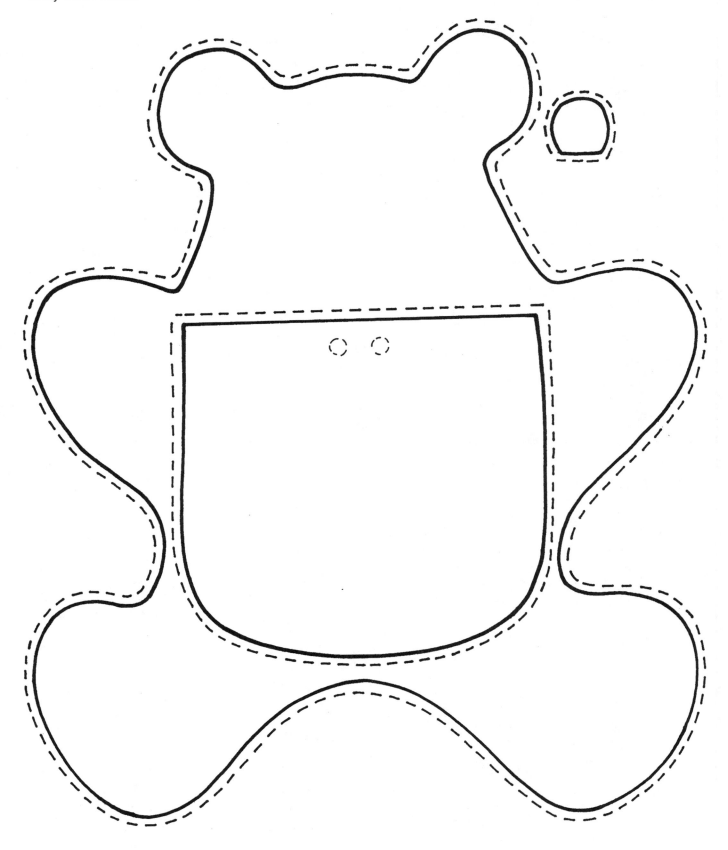

Welcome Ruler and Wreath

Liven things up during your study of measurement by using gingerbread people. Take a break from the math book and get the children interested in using measuring tools with this hands-on activity. Children will make this welcome craft with either a ruler or a tape measure. Discuss the various markings on each as the children work!

Welcome Ruler
Materials needed:
- patterns on pages 125–126
- large bow
- ½in. (13 mm) wide ribbon
- yardstick or meterstick
- colored construction paper
- tan card stock
- decorative items: ric-rac, wiggle eyes
- crayons or markers
- glue
- scissors

Directions:
1. Attach a bow to the center of a 2 ft. (61 cm) length of ribbon.
2. Tie the ends of the ribbon to the yardstick as shown so that it is balanced.
3. Using the patterns provided, (enlarge if desired) cut the word "Welcome" from colored construction paper and glue it to the front of the yardstick or meterstick.
4. Reproduce one gingerbread person pattern onto tan card stock paper for each child. Have the children write their names on the center of their gingerbread people and decorate it with ric-rac, wiggle eyes, crayons, and markers.
5. Glue one end of varied lengths of ribbon to the back of each personalized gingerbread person. Glue the other end of the ribbon to the back of the yardstick.

Tape Measure Wall Wreath
Create this wreath for larger classes. Use the same materials on the list above, except omit the ruler and replace the bow with a tape measure bow. You will also need poster board or cardboard.

Directions:
1. Cut a large wreath shape out of poster board or cardboard that is big enough to accommodate a gingerbread man for each child. Attach a ribbon loop to the top to serve as a hanger.
2. Using the pattern, reproduce one gingerbread person for each child onto tan card stock. Let the children write their names on the center of their patterns and decorate them with ric-rac, wiggle eyes, crayons, and markers.
3. Glue the completed gingerbread people to the wreath, overlapping slightly but not covering the names.
4. Fashion a large bow from a tape measure and attach it to the bottom of the wreath.

Shimmering Musical Notes

March is "Music in Our Schools Month." The craft below provides a nonmusical, yet artistic way, to remind students of the importance of music both in our schools and in our lives. The notes can be used to quiz students on their half, quarter, and eighth notes, as well as the treble and bass clefs.

Materials needed:
- ☺ 7 craft sticks
- ☺ black acrylic paint
- ☺ foam paintbrush
- ☺ patterns on page 128
- ☺ black construction paper
- ☺ glue
- ☺ silver glitter
- ☺ fishing line
- ☺ paper clip (optional)

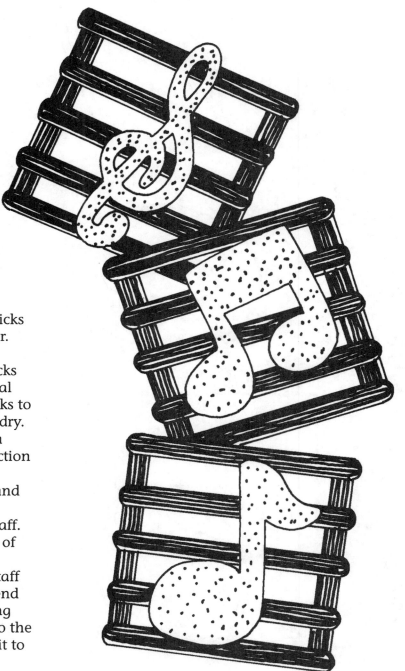

Directions:
1. Paint both sides of all seven craft sticks black. Let them dry on waxed paper.
2. Place two of the sticks vertically. Evenly space the remaining five sticks horizontally between the two vertical sticks. Glue each end of the five sticks to the first two as shown. Let the glue dry.
3. Using the patterns provided, trace a musical symbol onto black construction paper and cut it out.
4. Spread glue evenly on the symbol and cover it with glitter. Let it dry.
5. Glue the symbol to the craft stick staff.
6. Use spray glitter to cover both sides of the staff.
7. Tie a fishing line to the top of the staff to serve as a hanger. Tie the other end of the line to a light fixture or ceiling hanger. If needed, tie a paper clip to the end of the fishing line and untwist it to make a hook for hanging the staff.

One Hundred Day Mask

For some reason, celebrating the 100th day of school seems to be a favorite activity of children. Of course you can include traditional activities such as having the children bring 100 of an edible item for a snack or line up 100 children for a photo. However, for a nontraditional celebration idea, have your students create these special masks. Children will enjoy personalizing, and then modeling, their creations. Be sure to take photographs of the results!

Materials needed:
- 100-day mask pattern on page 130
- white card stock
- markers or crayons
- scissors
- glue
- glitter glue

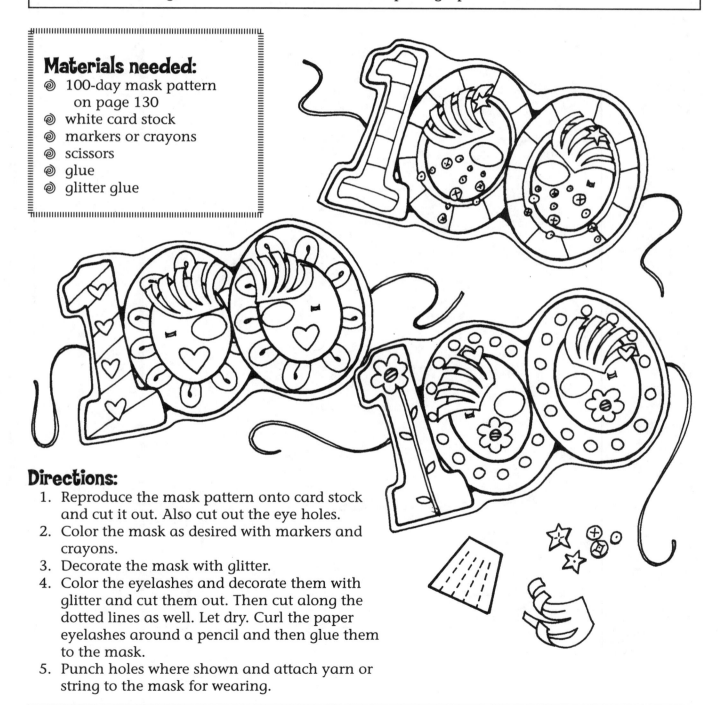

Directions:
1. Reproduce the mask pattern onto card stock and cut it out. Also cut out the eye holes.
2. Color the mask as desired with markers and crayons.
3. Decorate the mask with glitter.
4. Color the eyelashes and decorate them with glitter and cut them out. Then cut along the dotted lines as well. Let dry. Curl the paper eyelashes around a pencil and then glue them to the mask.
5. Punch holes where shown and attach yarn or string to the mask for wearing.

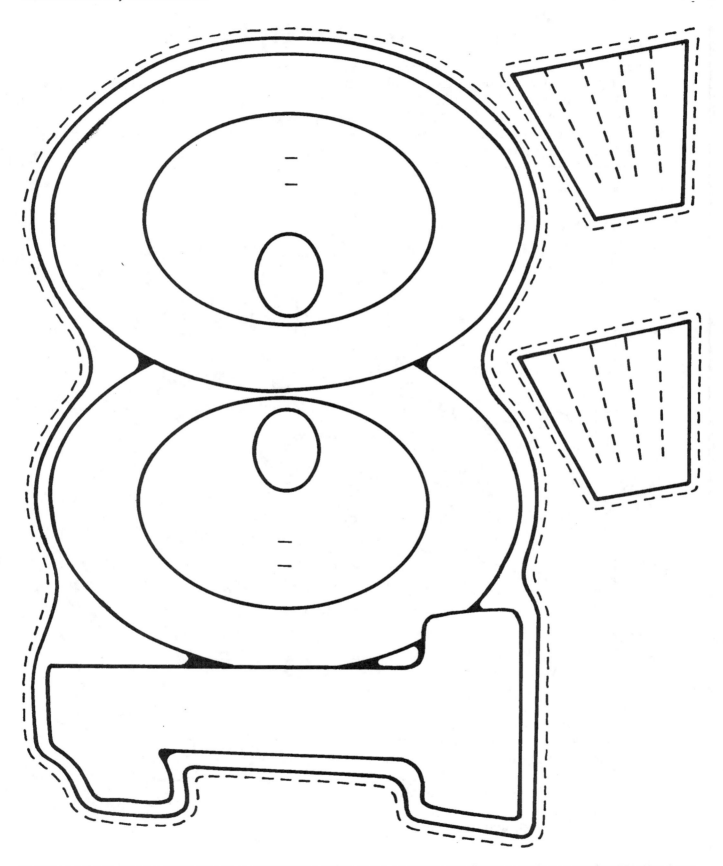

Patriotic Star Wreath

This patriotic star wreath is not only easy and fun to make, but it can be used as a colorful classroom decoration for Veterans Day. Make the wreaths a week before Veterans Day to display in the classroom. Then, for the holiday itself, have the children take their wreaths home and give them to veterans in their families. Alternatively, your class could take the wreaths to veterans living in a local nursing home or donate them to a local VFW.

Materials needed:
- ◎ star patterns on page 132
- ◎ white poster board
- ◎ red, white, and blue construction paper
- ◎ red, white, and blue ribbon
- ◎ red, white, and blue glitter
- ◎ star stickers in a patriotic color mix
- ◎ craft glue
- ◎ scissors
- ◎ paper punch

Directions:
1. Draw a circle 10 in. (25 cm) in diameter with a 6 in. (15 cm) center onto poster board. Cut out the center hole and use it as the base of the wreath.
2. Reproduce the star pattern page onto red, white, and blue paper and cut out the stars.
3. Glue stars of different sizes and colors on top of each other to create striped patterns if desired. Decorate the stars with glitter glue. Punch two holes in the center of the larger stars. Thread colored ribbons through the holes and tie the bows.
4. Space the larger stars with bows evenly around the wreath and glue in place. Fill the spaces in between them with smaller stars.
5. Complete the wreath by decorating it with star stickers. Punch a hole at the top of the wreath and add a cord to serve as a hanger.

Veterans Day Picture Frame

Another wonderful way to honor veterans is to have the children create special picture frames to display photographs of veterans in their families. Have each child create the patriotic frame described below to highlight a very special veteran.

Materials needed:
◎ photograph or photocopy of photo
◎ cardboard or poster board
◎ pencil
◎ clear plastic sheets
◎ red, white, or blue plastic lacing cord
◎ paper punch
◎ scissors
◎ decorative items: star stickers, star sequins, or precut craft foam sheets

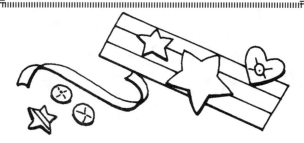

Directions:
1. Decide on a shape for your frame, making sure its size is at least 2 in. (5 cm) larger than the photo on all sides. Draw the shape on a piece of cardboard and cut it out. This is your pattern. Use the pattern to cut out two matching pieces of plastic.
2. Hold the two pieces of plastic together and punch holes evenly spaced around the outer edge.
3. Glue the photo to the center of one of the plastic shapes.
4. Decorate around the photo with stickers, sequins, or precut craft foam shapes, taking care not to cover any of the punched holes with the decorations.
5. Place the second plastic shape on top, making sure to match the holes. Lace the two sheets together with plastic lacing cord. Secure the ends by tying them together with a knot.

Star Door Decoration

Vary the colors of this eye-catching door decoration to alter its purpose. Use red, white, and blue for Veterans Day, Flag Day, or Independence Day decorations, or make a bright yellow star trailed by rainbow colors of streamers for a door decor that can be used all year.

Materials needed:
- star patterns on page 135
- cardboard
- glue
- yellow felt
- assorted colors of sparkly chenille stems
- pencil
- assorted colors of construction paper
- scissors
- paper streamers—
  red, yellow, blue, and green
- 2 wiggle eyes
- pink pom-pom
- fine-point marker
- bold marker
- cord or ribbon for hanging
- assorted shape sequins if desired

Directions:
1. Cover the large cardboard star base with yellow paper or felt.
2. Make a face on the star by gluing on the wiggle eyes and a pom-pom nose. Draw a mouth with the black marker.
3. Cut colorful stars from construction paper using the patterns provided. Glue the stars to the ends of chenille stems. Wrap some of the chenille stems around a pencil to make them curly. Glue the completed stems to the back of the cardboard star as shown in the illustration.
4. Cut out four different colored long streamers. Glue a star at one end of each streamer and attach the other end to the back of the star.
5. Using a wide marker, write the family name on the front of the star.
6. Glue sequins to the star for additional sparkle if desired.
7. Punch a hole at the top of the star and attach a cord through it to serve as a hanger.

3-D Patriotic Star

Children add depth to their art when they create this 3-D star. In red, white, and blue it makes a great decoration to hang from the ceiling for Flag Day, Veterans Day, Independence Day, or Patriot Day.

Materials needed:
- ◎ star patterns on page 137
- ◎ red, white, and blue construction paper
- ◎ red, white, and blue tissue paper or streamers
- ◎ red, white, blue, silver star stickers
- ◎ red markers or crayons
- ◎ yarn: red, white, or blue
- ◎ scissors
- ◎ glue

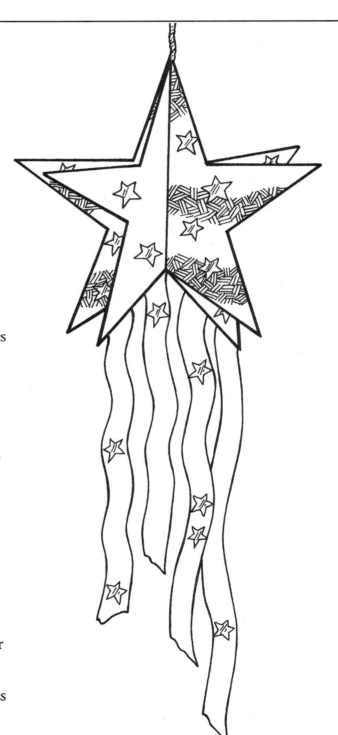

Directions:
1. Using Pattern A as a guide, cut out two stars from white construction paper.
2. Glue a long piece of yarn to the top of one of the white stars. Glue the other white star on top of the first, sandwiching the yarn in between them as shown in figure 1.
3. Color red stripes on both sides of the star.
4. Cut a slit on the bottom of the white star as indicated on Pattern A.
5. Using Pattern B as a guide, cut one red and one blue star.
6. Cut narrow streamers about ¾ in. (19 mm) wide from tissue paper or crepe paper. Glue one end of each streamer onto the bottom edge of the red star as shown in figure 2.
7. Glue the blue star on top of the red one, sandwiching the streamers in between them.
8. Cut a slit on the top of the red and blue star as indicated on Pattern B.
9. To make the 3-D star, slide the white star down into the slit in the red and blue star as shown.
10. Finish decorating the star with the stickers.

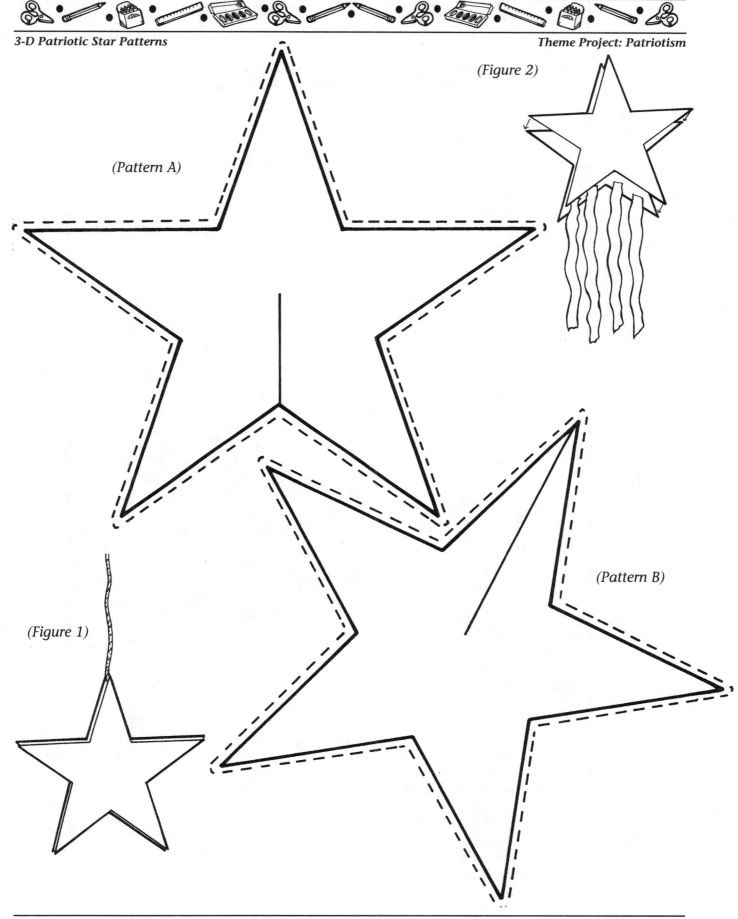

(Figure 2)

(Pattern A)

(Pattern B)

(Figure 1)

Theme Project: Patriotism

Flag Decoration

These bright tissue paper flags can be used to decorate anywhere in your school, but they will look especially breath taking when displayed in a number of windows that are close together. The flags may be used as door, wall, or window decorations or as refrigerator magnets when magnetic strips are attached to their back.

Materials needed:
- ◎ 9 in. x 12 in. (23 cm x 30 cm) cardboard
- ◎ blue tempera paint
- ◎ paintbrushes
- ◎ pencil
- ◎ water cup
- ◎ paper towels
- ◎ popcorn or foam packing peanuts
- ◎ red and white tissue paper
- ◎ glue
- ◎ string or magnetic strips

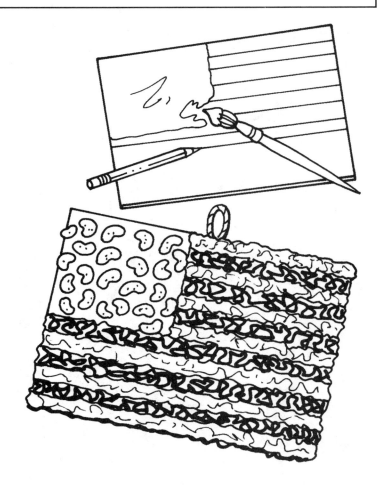

Directions:
1. Using a pencil, draw an American flag design on the cardboard.
2. Cover the work area with newspaper. Paint the square on the upper left corner of the cardboard blue and let dry.
3. Glue popcorn or packing foam peanuts to the blue square to represent the stars.
4. Crumple red and white tissue paper into small balls and glue them onto the flag to form red and white stripes. Let the glue dry.
5. Attach a string to serve as a hanger, or add magnetic strips to make a large refrigerator magnet.

Pet Shop Memory Match

It is always fun to test your memory by trying to recall what is hidden behind a panel. In this memory matching game the children will determine which pet hides behind each window of the pet shop. The best feature about this activity is that the children get to create the game materials. Afterwards, each child can have their own version of the game to play with their parents or friends.

Materials needed:
- patterns on pages 140-142 and 144
- white card stock
- felt or fabric pieces (precut) 1 ¾ in. x 2 in. (44 mm x 50 mm)
- utility knife
- restickable adhesive
- crayons or colored markers
- masking tape
- glue sticks
- envelope
- scissors

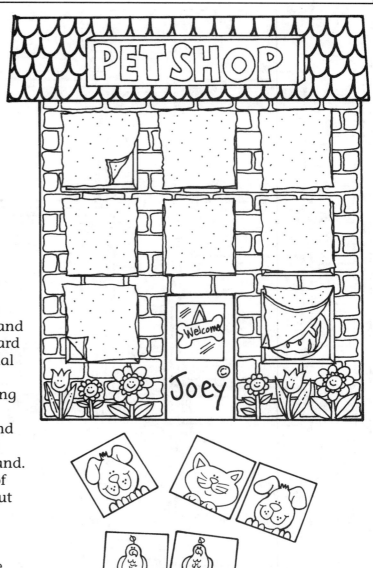

Directions:
1. Reproduce the pet shop building (page 140–141) and roof pattern (page 144) and animals cards (page 142) onto white card stock. Color the building and the animal pairs. Instruct the children to color the animal pairs to match or draw matching pairs of animals on the blank cards provided. Cut out the building, roof, and the animal cards. Cut out the building windows for younger children beforehand.

2. Run a line of glue along the top edge of each pet shop window and glue a precut fabric or felt piece over the window to make a curtain.

3. Tape the front of the building and the back of the building together along the top edge with masking tape. Glue the roof along the top edge to cover the masking tape hinge.

4. Glue an envelope to the back of the game board for storing the animal cards.

5. Apply restickable adhesive to the back of the animals cutouts.

Pet Shop Pocket

For most children, there is nothing more important than the desire to own a pet. With this pet shop pocket, even those children whose parents do not allow pets at home will be able to have a "pet" of their own. Puppies, kittens, and turtles are just some of the animals available at the pet shop. A child can choose a favorite animal, give it a name, and keep it safe at the pet shop with all of the other pets!

Materials needed:
- ◎ patterns on pages 144-147
- ◎ file folder
- ◎ white card stock
- ◎ stapler
- ◎ craft sticks
- ◎ glue
- ◎ scissors
- ◎ markers or crayons
- ◎ small wiggle eyes
- ◎ feathers, yarn scraps, cotton balls, tiny pom-poms

Directions:
1. Draw a line across the front center of the file folder. (See figure 1.) All diagrams for the construction of the file folder are found on page 144.
2. Cut off the top half of the front panel of the file folder. (See figure 2.)
3. Draw a line 2 in. (5 cm) from the top of the inside of the file folder. Cut along the line to form a flap. (See figure 3.)
4. Fold the flap down. (See figure 4.)
5. Run a line of glue along the edge of the inside bottom and side, gluing the front and back panels together to form an envelope. Reinforce the edge by stapling along the same edge.
6. Reproduce the pet shop and animal patterns onto white card stock and cut them out. Color the patterns as desired.
7. Glue the roof to the envelope flap and the store to the front of the envelope.
8. Color the pets and glue them to the top of the craft sticks. Decorate the pets with wiggle eyes, yarn tails, hair, and whiskers; cotton ball tail for bunnies; fur for the mouse; feathers for the birds; and, pom-pom noses. Store all the animals inside the pet shop.

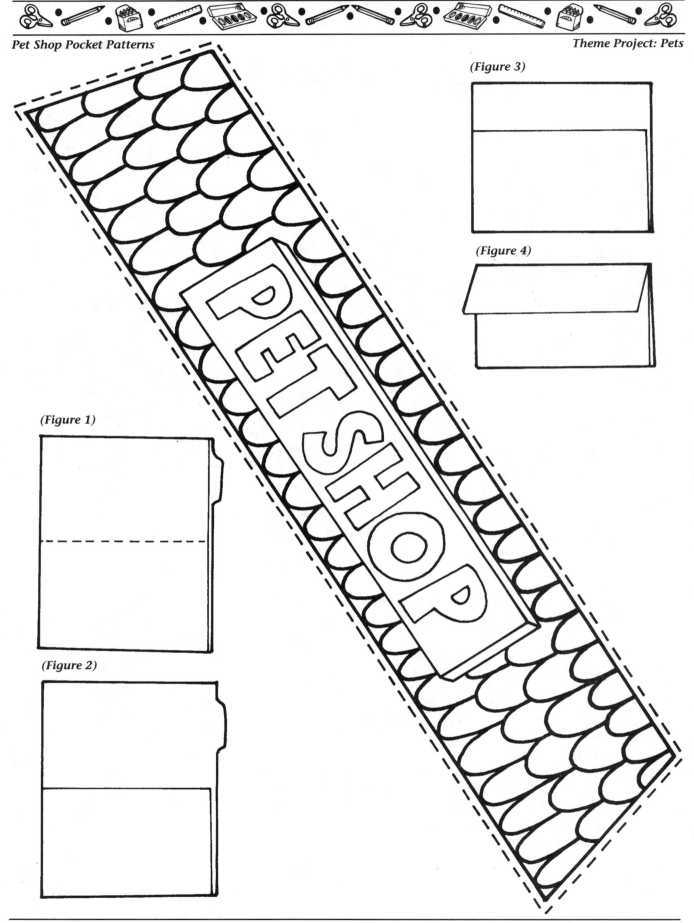

(Figure 3)

(Figure 4)

(Figure 1)

(Figure 2)

FISH FOOD

Ocean Adventure Tank

This aquarium will be filled with sea life and items from the seashore and will liven up any lesson on fish or the ocean. Sequined paper fish with wiggle eyes can be seen "swimming" behind the cellophane "glass" front of the aquarium. Encourage the children to be creative as they add seaweed, shells, sea horses, or tiny starfish cutouts to their creations.

Materials needed:

◎ patterns on pages 149-150
◎ shoe box, oatmeal box, or an ice-cream container
◎ white card stock
◎ children's photos
◎ plastic wrap
◎ masking tape
◎ colored markers or crayons
◎ glitter markers, sequins, wiggle eyes
◎ scissors
◎ string
◎ glue
◎ artificial plants
◎ seashells, driftwood, or sticks
◎ sandpaper sheets or clean dry sand

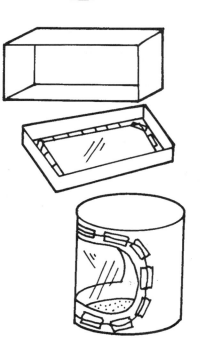

Directions:

1. Reproduce the patterns onto white card stock.
2. Prepare fish tank boxes as shown on the right.
3. Cut a piece of sandpaper to cover the bottom of the fish tank box and glue it in place. Alternatively, spread glue on the inside bottom of the box and then sprinkle with sand.
4. Color the patterns and decorate as desired. Glue photos of the children's faces on the divers. Cut out the patterns.
5. Glue some of the decorated patterns to the interior sides and bottom of the fish tank along with adding artificial plants, driftwood, sticks, and seashells. Select some of the fish tank creatures and attach them to strings and hang them from the lid of the fish tank container.
6. Complete the aquarium by decorating the exterior with crayons or markers.

Styrofoam Solar System

Teach children about space by making a model of the solar system using paint, craft wire, and Styrofoam balls. As the children each build their own solar system, talk about the names of the planets and their positions in relation to the sun. Offer encyclopedia or textbook pictures for the children to view while they are arranging their planets.

Materials needed:
- large Styrofoam ball
- a variety of smaller Styrofoam balls
- craft wire
- wire cutters
- assorted acrylic paints
- water pans
- paintbrushes
- paper towels
- colored yarn
- glue
- gold glitter
- newspaper
- string

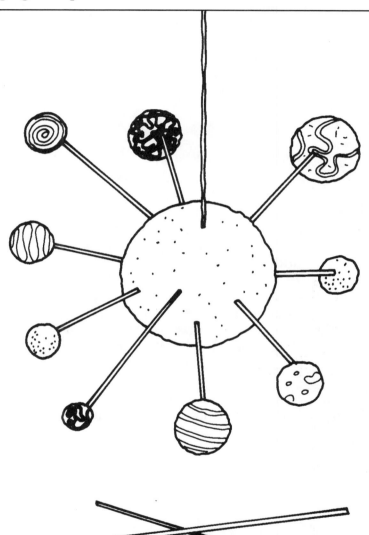

Directions:
1. Cover the work area with newspaper. Paint the large Styrofoam ball yellow and sprinkle it with gold glitter. This is the sun and the center of the solar system.
2. Decorate one Styrofoam ball for each planet. Refer to pictures of the solar system to compare actual sizes (biggest to smallest), colors, rings, etc. Decorate the planets with paint or by coating the balls with glue and wrapping with colored yarn. (You may only want to wrap Saturn in yarn to represent its rings.)
3. When the planets are completed, determine their position from the sun and cut craft wire accordingly. Put a dab of glue on each end of the wire. Poke one end into the sun and the other end into the appropriate planet.
4. Attach a string to serve as a hanger.

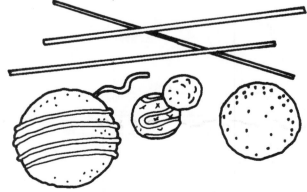

Giant Wristwatch

Learning to tell time is a special rite of passage for primary-aged school children. For some children learning to tell time may be a breeze, while others will struggle to understand the concept. Make learning to tell time a positive experience by having each child create their own giant wristwatch.

Materials needed:
- ◉ patterns on page 153
- ◉ construction paper
- ◉ white card stock
- ◉ paper fastener
- ◉ glue
- ◉ crayons, markers, glitter glue

Directions:
1. Reproduce the patterns onto white card stock. Cut out the clock face, hands, and buckle. Color and decorate as desired.
2. Cut a sheet of construction paper in half as shown below. Glue the two strips together at one end to form the wristband.
3. Trim one end of the wristband to a point as shown and glue the buckle to the other end.
4. Center the clock face on the band and glue it in place.
5. Punch a small hole through the center of the clock face and through the clock hands. Attach the clock hands to the clock face with a paper fastener.

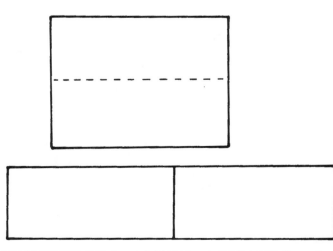

My Zoo

Children and adults alike love animals and zoos. Children will enjoy creating these zoo animals to have as their own. To add educational value, discuss each animals' natural environment. Also talk about how its camouflage (coloring, dots, stripes, etc.) protects the animal and helps it survive in the wild.

Zoo
Materials needed:
- ◎ zoo box patterns on pages 159-160
- ◎ cardboard box (an instant oatmeal box or one of similar size)
- ◎ white paper
- ◎ white card stock
- ◎ crayons or markers
- ◎ assorted colors of chenille stems
- ◎ artificial flowers
- ◎ 2 tiny wiggle eyes
- ◎ glue
- ◎ scissors

Zoo Animals
Materials needed:
- ◎ animal patterns on pages 155-158
- ◎ assorted texture and print fabric, felt, fur, vinyl, feathers, quilt batting
- ◎ colorful paper
- ◎ sandpaper
- ◎ card stock paper
- ◎ craft sticks
- ◎ small wiggle eyes (optional)
- ◎ yarn, felt, and chenille scraps
- ◎ tiny pom-poms or beads
- ◎ glue
- ◎ scissors

Directions:
1. Reproduce the stone wall pattern on white paper. Copy as many as needed to cover the entire box.
2. Reproduce the zoo sign, door, windows, palm tree, and plants onto card stock paper.
3. Glue the stone wall pattern to the sides of the box.
4. Color the patterns on the card stock with markers or crayons and cut out.
5. Decorate your zoo box with the colored cut outs, the artificial flower blossoms, and leaves.
6. Punch two holes in the top of the box as shown and attach a chenille stem handle.
7. To create the snake that is shown on the zoo box handle, use a 6 in. (15 cm) long green chenille stem. Glue the wiggle eyes to the loop and twist your snake around the zoo box handle.

Directions:
1. Reproduce the animal patterns onto card stock and cut out.
2. Pick an appropriate color, textured fabric, or paper for each animal.
3. Glue the animal shape to the back of the fabric or paper and cut out the shape.
4. Glue a craft stick to the back of each animal.
5. Decorate each zoo animal by adding details for the face, nose, ears, whiskers, hair, and tail by using the craft materials listed above.

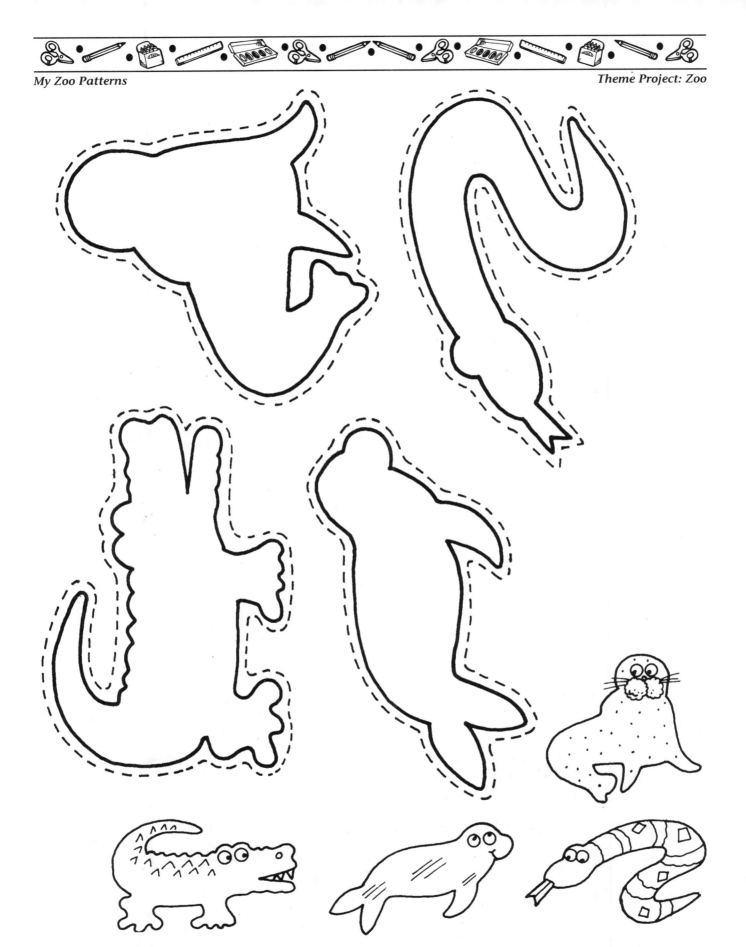

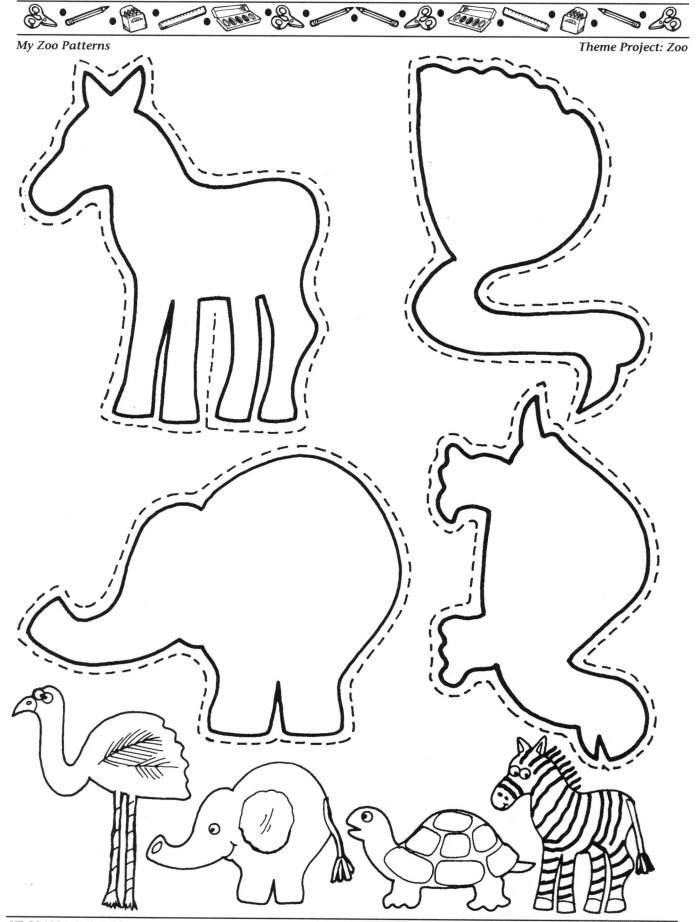